W9-DAD-852

Fodor's

Pocket
Barbados

Reprinted from *Fodor's Caribbean*

Fodor's Travel Publications, Inc.
New York • Toronto • London • Sydney • Auckland
www.fodors.com/

Fodor's Pocket Barbados

EDITORS: Caroline Haberfeld and Christina Knight

Editorial Contributors: Robert Andrews, David Brown, Sunny Delaney, Heidi Sarna, Helayne Schiff, M. T. Schwartzman, Dinah A. Spritzer, Jane E. Zarem

Editorial Production: Laura M. Kidder

Maps: David Lindroth, *cartographer*; Robert Blake, *map editor*

Design: Fabrizio La Rocca, *creative director*; Lyndell Brookhouse-Gil, *cover design*; Jolie Novak, *photo editor*

Production/Manufacturing: Rebecca Zeiler

Cover Photograph: Andre Gallant/Image Bank

Copyright

Special Sales

Fodor's Travel Publications are available at special discounts for bulk purchases for sales promotions or premiums. Special editions can be created in large quantities for special needs. For more information, contact Special Markets, Fodor's Travel Publications, 201 E. 50th St., New York, NY 10022. Inquiries from Canada should be directed to Random House of Canada, Ltd., Marketing Dept., 1265 Aerowood Dr., Mississauga, Ont. L4W 1B9. Inquiries from the United Kingdom should be sent to Fodor's Travel Publications, 20 Vauxhall Bridge Rd., London SW1V 2SA, England.

PRINTED IN THE UNITED STATES OF AMERICA

10 9 8 7 6 5 4 3 2 1

CONTENTS

Maps and Plans

ON THE ROAD WITH FODOR'S

WE'RE ALWAYS thrilled to get letters from readers, especially one like this:

It took us an hour to decide what book to buy and we now know we picked the best one. Your book was wonderful, easy to follow, very accurate, and good on pointing out eating places, informal as well as formal. When we saw other people using your book, we would look at each other and smile.

Our editors and writers are deeply committed to making every Fodor's guide "the best one"— not only accurate but always charming, brimming with sound recommendations and solid ideas, right on the mark in describing restaurants and hotels, and full of fascinating facts that make you view what you've traveled to see in a rich new light.

About Our Writer

Our success in achieving our goals—and in helping to make your trip the best of all possible vacations—is a credit to the hard work of our writer.

Jane E. Zarem is a freelance writer from Connecticut who travels frequently to the Caribbean. Among the score of islands she has explored, she finds it difficult to pick a favorite—she loves them all. She is a member of the New York Travel Writers' Association and the International Food, Wine & Travel Writers' Association, and has contributed to numerous Fodor's guides, among them *New England USA, Cape Cod, Bahamas,* and *Great American Sports and Adventure Vacations,* as well as *Caribbean.*

New This Year

We're proud to announce that the American Society of Travel Agents has endorsed Fodor's as its guidebook of choice. ASTA is the world's largest and most influential travel trade association, operating in more than 170 countries, with 27,000 members pledged to adhere to a strict code of ethics reflecting the Society's motto, "Integrity in Travel." ASTA shares Fodor's devotion to providing smart, honest travel information and advice to travelers, and we've long recommended that our readers consult ASTA member agents for the experience and professionalism they bring to the table.

On the Web, check out Fodor's site (www.fodors.com/) for information on major destinations around the world and travel-savvy inter-active features. The Web site also lists the 85-plus radio stations nationwide that carry the *Fodor's Travel Show,* a live call-in program that airs every weekend. Tune in to hear guests discuss their wonderful adventures—or call in for answers to your most pressing travel questions.

How to Use This Book

Organization

Up front is **Essential Information,** an easy-to-use section divided alphabetically by topic. Under each listing you'll find tips and information that will help you accomplish what you need to in Barbados. You'll also find addresses and telephone numbers of organizations and companies that offer destination-related services and detailed information and publications.

The first chapter in the guide, **Destination: Barbados,** helps get you in the mood for your trip and alerts you to festivals and seasonal events you'll want to seek out.

The **chapters** in this book cover lodging, dining, beaches, outdoor activities and sports, shopping, nightlife, and exploring, and cruising to Barbados.

Icons and Symbols

★   Our special recommendations
✕   Restaurant
🖭   Lodging establishment
☾   Good for kids (rubber duckie)

☞   Sends you to another section of the guide for more information
✉   Address
☏   Telephone number
FAX Fax number
🕓   Opening and closing times
💰   Admission prices (those we give apply to adults; substantially reduced fees are almost always available for children, students, and senior citizens)

Hotel Facilities

We always list the facilities that are available—but we don't specify whether they cost extra: When pricing accommodations, always ask what's included. In addition, assume that all rooms have private baths unless otherwise noted.

There are numerous meal plans offered in Barbados: **European Plan** (EP, with no meals), **Full American Plan** (FAP, with all meals), **Modified American Plan** (MAP, with breakfast and dinner daily), **Continental Plan** (CP, with a Continental breakfast daily), or **all-inclusive** (all meals and most activities). At the end of each review, we have listed the meal plans the hotel offers.

A FAP is ideal if you're on a budget and don't want to worry about additional expenses. If, however, you enjoy a different dining experience each night, book rooms on the EP. Since some hotels insist on the MAP, particularly during high season, find out whether you can exchange dinner for lunch or for meals at neighboring hotels.

Restaurant Reservations and Dress Codes

Reservations are always a good idea; we note only when they're essential or when they are not accepted. Book as far ahead as you can, and reconfirm when you get to town. Unless otherwise noted, the restaurants listed are open daily for lunch and dinner. We mention dress only when men are required to wear a jacket or a jacket and tie.

Credit Cards

The following abbreviations are used: **AE**, American Express; **D**, Discover; **DC**, Diners Club; **MC**, MasterCard; and **V**, Visa.

Don't Forget to Write

You can use this book in the confidence that all prices and opening times are based on information supplied to us at press time; Fodor's cannot accept responsibility for any errors. Time inevitably brings changes, so always confirm information when it matters—especially if you're making a detour to visit a specific place. In addition, when making reservations be sure to mention if you have a disability or are traveling with children, if you prefer a private bath or a certain type of bed, or if you have specific dietary needs or other concerns.

Were the restaurants we recommended as described? Did our hotel picks exceed your expectations? Did you find a museum we recommended a waste of time? If you have complaints, we'll look into them and revise our entries when the facts warrant it. If you've discovered a special place that we haven't included, we'll pass the information along to our correspondents and have them check it out. So send us your feedback, positive *and* negative: E-mail us at editors@fodors.com (specifying the name of the book on the subject line) or write the Barbados editor at Fodor's, 201 East 50th Street, New York, New York 10022. Have a wonderful trip!

Karen Cure
Editorial Director

The Caribbean

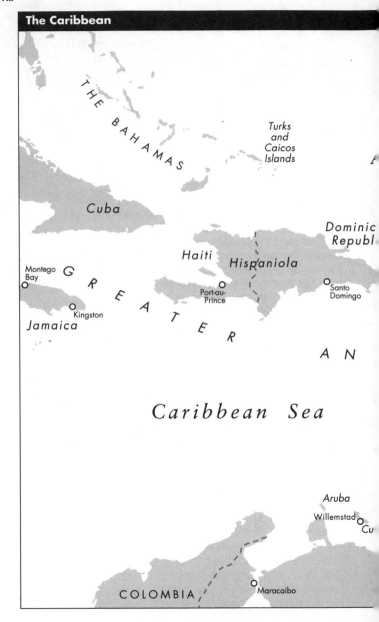

THE BAHAMAS

Turks
and
Caicos
Islands

Cuba

Dominic
Republ

Haiti   Hispaniola

Montego
Bay

G R E A T E R

Port-au-
Prince

Santo
Domingo

Kingston

Jamaica

A N

Caribbean Sea

Aruba

Willemstad   Cu

COLOMBIA   Maracaibo

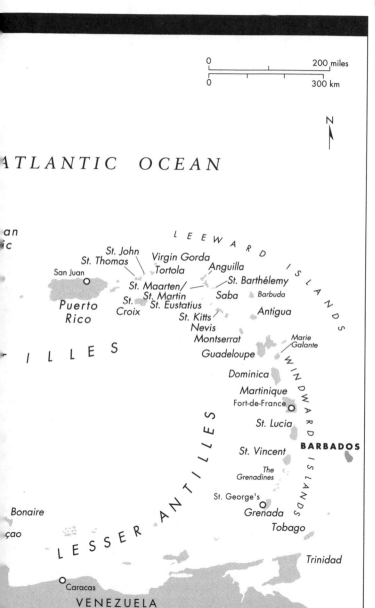

0 | 200 miles
0 | 300 km

N

ATLANTIC OCEAN

an
ic

St. John
St. Thomas   Virgin Gorda
Tortola   Anguilla
San Juan   St. Barthélemy
St. Maarten/   Saba   Barbuda
St.   St. Martin
Croix   St. Eustatius
Puerto   St. Kitts
Rico   Nevis
                    Montserrat
                                    Marie
                                    Galante
                    Guadeloupe

LEEWARD ISLANDS

Antigua

- ILLES

Dominica

Martinique
Fort-de-France

St. Lucia

WINDWARD ISLANDS

BARBADOS

St. Vincent

The
Grenadines

St. George's
Grenada

Tobago

Bonaire

çao

LESSER ANTILLES

LESSER ANTILLES

Trinidad

Caracas
VENEZUELA

x

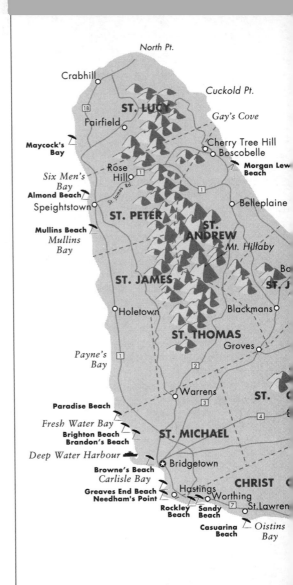

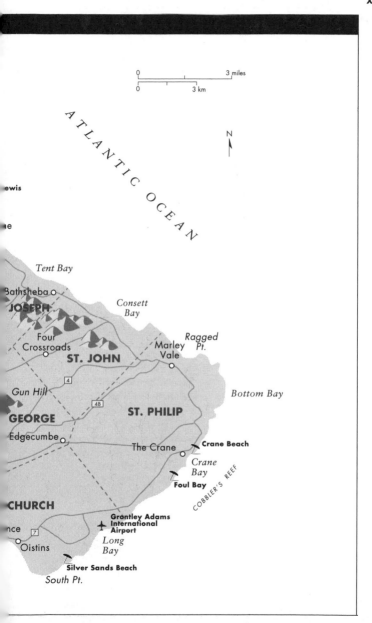

0   3 miles

0   3 km

N

A T L A N T I C   O C E A N

ewis

ne

Tent Bay

Bathsheba ○

JOSEPH

Consett Bay

Four
Crossroads ○

ST. JOHN

Marley
Vale ○

*Ragged
Pt.*

4

Gun Hill

4B

ST. PHILIP

Bottom Bay

GEORGE

Edgecumbe ○

The Crane ○

Crane Beach

*Crane
Bay*

COBBLER'S REEF

Foul Bay

CHURCH

nce

7

○ Oistins

**Grantley Adams
International
Airport**

*Long
Bay*

Silver Sands Beach

South Pt.

ESSENTIAL INFORMATION

Basic Information on Traveling in Barbados, Savvy Tips to Make Your Trip a Breeze, and Companies and Organizations to Contact

AIR TRAVEL

AIRLINES➤ **American Airlines** (☎ 246/428–4170 or 800/433–7300) and **BWIA** (☎ 246/426–2111 or 800/538–2942) both have nonstop flights from New York and direct flights from Miami. **American Eagle** (☎ 246/428–4170 or 800/433–7300) serves Barbados from other U.S. cities with connecting flights through San Juan. **Air Jamaica** (☎ 800/523–5585) has daily nonstop service from New York.

Interisland service is scheduled on **LIAT** (☎ 246/495–1187), **Air Martinique** (☎ 246/431–0540), and **BWIA** (☎ 246/426–2111); **Air St. Vincent/Air Mustique** (☎ 246/428–1638) links Barbados with St. Vincent and the Grenadines.

FROM CANADA➤ **Air Canada** (☎ 246/428–5077 or 800/776–3000) flies nonstop from Toronto.

FROM THE U.K.➤ **British Airways** (☎ 0345/222–111) has nonstop service, and **British West Indian Airways** (☎ 0181/570–5552) connects through Trinidad.

THE LOWEST FARE

The least-expensive airfares to Barbados are priced for round-trip travel. Major airlines usually require that you book far in advance and stay at least seven days and no more than 30 to get the lowest fares. Ask about "ultra-saver" fares, which are the cheapest; they must be booked 90 days in advance and are nonrefundable. A little more expensive are "super-saver" fares, which require only a 30-day advance purchase. Remember that penalties for refunds or scheduling changes are stiffer for international tickets, usually about $150. International flights are also sensitive to the season: **plan to fly in the off season** for the cheapest fares. If your destination or home city has more than one gateway, **compare prices to and from different airports.** Also price flights scheduled for off-peak hours, which may be significantly less expensive.

To save money on flights from the United Kingdom and back, **look into an APEX or Super-PEX ticket.** APEX tickets must be booked in advance and have certain restrictions. Super-PEX tickets can be purchased at the airport on the day of departure—subject to availability.

AGENTS

Travel agents, especially those who specialize in finding the lowest fares, can be especially helpful when booking a plane ticket. When you're quoted a price, **ask your agent if the price is likely to get any lower.** Good agents know the seasonal fluctuations of airfares and can usually anticipate a sale or fare war. However, waiting can be risky: The fare could go *up* as seats become scarce, and you may wait so long that your preferred flight sells out. A wait-and-see strategy works best if your plans are flexible, but if you must arrive and depart on certain dates, don't delay.

CONSOLIDATORS

Consolidators buy tickets for scheduled flights at reduced rates from the airlines then sell them at prices that beat the best fare available directly from the airlines, usually without advance restrictions. Sometimes you can even get your money back if you need to return the ticket. Carefully read the fine print detailing penalties for changes and cancellations, and **confirm your consolidator reservation with the airline.**

CONSOLIDATORS➤ **United States Air Consolidators Association** (✉ 925 L St., Suite 220, Sacramento,

CA 95814, ☎ 916/441–4166, FAX 916/441–3520).

BUMPING

Airlines routinely overbook planes, knowing that not everyone with a ticket will show up, but sometimes everyone does. When that happens, airlines ask for volunteers to give up their seats. In return these volunteers usually get a certificate for a free flight and are rebooked on the next flight out. If there are not enough volunteers the airline must choose who will be denied boarding. The first to get bumped are passengers who checked in late and those flying on discounted tickets, so **get to the gate and check in as early as possible,** especially during peak periods.

Always **bring a photo ID to the airport.** You may be asked to show it before you are allowed to check in.

ENJOY THE FLIGHT

For more legroom, **request an emergency-aisle seat;** don't however, sit in the row in front of the emergency aisle or in front of a bulkhead, where seats may not recline. If you don't like airline food, **ask for special meals when booking.** These can be vegetarian, low-cholesterol, or kosher, for example. Some carriers have prohibited smoking throughout their systems; others allow smoking only on certain routes or even certain departures from that route, so **contact your carrier regarding its smoking policy.**

COMPLAINTS

If your baggage goes astray or your flight goes awry, complain right away. Most carriers require that you file a claim immediately.

AIRLINE COMPLAINTS➤ U.S. Department of Transportation **Aviation Consumer Protection Division** (⊠ C-75, Room 4107, Washington, DC 20590, ☎ 202/366–2220). **Federal Aviation Administration (FAA) Consumer Hotline** (☎ 800/322–7873).

AIRPORTS

The **Grantley Adams International Airport** (☎ 246/428–7101) in Christ Church is 4 hours and 20 minutes from New York and 3½ hours from Miami.

TRANSFERS

Airport taxis are not metered. A large sign at the airport announces the fixed rate to each hotel or parish, stated in both Barbados and U.S. dollars (about $28 to Speightstown, $20 to West Coast hotels, $10–$13 to South Coast ones). The Adams-Barrow-Cummins (ABC) Highway bypasses Bridgetown, which saves time getting to the West Coast.

BICYCLE & SCOOTER RENTALS

Bicycles rent for about $10 a day, or $50 per week, with a $50 refundable deposit. Scooters rent for about $31 a day for two-seaters, with a $100 refundable deposit. Both are for rent at **FunSeekers**

(⊠ Main Rd., Rockley, Christ Church, ☎ 246/435–8206).

BOATING

YACHT CHARTERS➤ **Alden Yacht Charters** (⊠ 1909 Alden Landing, Portsmouth, RI 02871, ☎ 401/683–1782 or 800/662–2628, FAX 401/683–3668). **Huntley Yacht Vacations** (⊠ 210 Preston Rd., Wernersville, PA 19565, ☎ 610/678–2628 or 800/322–9224, FAX 610/670–1767). **Lynn Jachney Charters** (⊠ Box 302, Marblehead, MA 01945, ☎ 617/639–0787 or 800/223–2050, FAX 617/639–0216). **Nicholson Yacht Charters** (⊠ 78 Bolton St., Cambridge, MA 02140-3321, ☎ 617/661–0555 or 800/662–6066, FAX 617/661–0554). **Ocean Voyages** (⊠ 1709 Bridgeway, Sausalito, CA 94965, ☎ 415/332–4681 or 800/299–4444, FAX 415/332–7460). **Russell Yacht Charters** (⊠ 404 Hulls Hwy., #175, Southport, CT 06490, ☎ 203/255–2783 or 800/635–8895). **SailAway Yacht Charters** (⊠ 15605 S.W. 92nd Ave., Miami, FL 33157-1972, ☎ 305/253–7245 or 800/724–5292, FAX 305/251–4408).

BUS TRAVEL

Buses, maxitaxis, and vans provide a great opportunity to experience local color, and your fellow passengers will be eager to share their advice. All cost Bds$1.50 for any destination and be sure to **bring exact change for the blue public buses,** which is appreciated on the private ones, too. Private transports include yellow buses with a blue stripe, maxitaxis, and the white ZR vans with a burgundy stripe. All travel constantly along Highway 1 (St. James Road) and Highway 7 (South Coast Main Road) and are plentiful, reliable, and usually packed. Bus stops are marked by small signs on roadside poles that say TO CITY or OUT OF CITY, meaning the direction relative to Bridgetown. Even if you're standing at the stop, **flag down the bus with your hand;** they don't always stop automatically.

CAR RENTAL

It's a pleasure to explore Barbados by car. Take time to study a map—although small signs tacked to trees and poles at intersections in the island's interior point the way to most attractions. The remote roads are in good repair, yet few are well lighted at night—and night falls quickly at about 6 PM. Even in full daylight, the tall sugarcane fields lining the road in interior sections can make visibility difficult. The speed limit, in keeping with the pace of life, is 37 mph in the country, 21 mph in town. Use caution: Pedestrians often walk in the roads. And remember: Drive on the left, and **be especially careful negotiating roundabouts (traffic circles).** Gas costs nearly $4 a gallon.

There are no major car-rental agencies in Barbados, but nearly 30 local operations rent cars (with

and without air-conditioning) or minimokes (open-air vehicles). The cost is about $75–$85 a day (or about $275–$285 a week), usually with a three- or four-day minimum. The fee generally includes insurance and a local driver's license. All rental companies provide pick-up and delivery service, offer unlimited mileage, and accept major credit cards.

LOCAL AGENCIES➤ **Dear's Garage** (✉ Christ Church, ☎ 246/429–9277 or 246/427–7853). **National** (✉ Bush Hall, St. Michael, ☎ 246/426–0603). **P&S Car Rentals** (✉ St. Michael, ☎ 246/424–2052). **Sunny Isle** (✉ Worthing, ☎ 246/435–7979). **Sunset Crest Rentals** (✉ St. James, ☎ 246/432–1482).

NEED INSURANCE?

When driving a rented car you are generally responsible for any damage to or loss of the vehicle. You also are liable for any property damage or personal injury that you may cause while driving. Before you rent, **see what coverage you already have** under the terms of your personal auto-insurance policy and credit cards.

BEWARE SURCHARGES

Before you pick up a car in one city and leave it in another, **ask about drop-off charges or one-way service fees,** which can be substantial. Note, too, that some rental agencies charge extra if you return the car before the time specified on your contract. To avoid a hefty refueling fee, **fill the tank just before you turn in the car,** but be aware that gas stations near the rental outlet may overcharge.

REQUIREMENTS

To rent a car you must have an international driver's license or Barbados driving permit, obtainable at the airport, police stations, and major car-rental firms for $5 if you have a valid driver's license.

CUSTOMS & DUTIES

When shopping, **keep receipts** for all of your purchases. Upon reentering the country, **be ready to show customs officials what you've bought.** If you feel a duty is incorrect, appeal the assessment. If you object to the way your clearance was handled, get the inspector's badge number. In either case, first ask to see a supervisor, then write to the port director at the address listed on your receipt. Send a copy of the receipt and other appropriate documentation. If you still don't get satisfaction you can take your case to customs headquarters in Washington.

ENTERING THE U.S.

You may bring home $600 worth of foreign goods duty-free if you've been out of the country for at least 48 hours and haven't used the $600 allowance or any part of it in the past 30 days. This allowance, higher than the standard $400 exemption, applies to Barba-

dos and the two dozen countries included in the Caribbean Basin Initiative (CBI). If you also visit a non-CBI country, such as Martinique, you may still bring in $600 worth of goods duty-free, but no more than $400 may be from the non-CBI country. If your travel includes the USVI a $1,200 allowance applies, but at least $600 worth of goods must be from the USVI.

Travelers 21 and older may bring back 1 liter of alcohol duty-free. In addition, regardless of your age, you are allowed 200 cigarettes and 100 non-Cuban cigars. (At press time, a federal rule restricting tobacco access to persons 18 years and older did not apply to importation.) Antiques, which the U.S. Customs Service defines as objects more than 100 years old, enter duty-free, as do original works of art done entirely by hand, including paintings, drawings, and sculptures.

You may also send packages home duty-free: up to $200 worth of goods for personal use, with a limit of one parcel per addressee per day (and no alcohol or tobacco products or perfume worth more than $5); label the package PERSONAL USE, and attach a list of its contents and their retail value. Do not label the package UNSOLICITED GIFT, or your duty-free exemption will drop to $100. Mailed items do not affect your duty-free allowance on your return.

INFORMATION➤ **U.S. Customs Service** (✉ Box 7407, Washington, DC 20044, ☎ 202/927–6724; complaints, ✉ Office of Regulations and Rulings, 1301 Constitution Ave. NW, Washington, DC 20229; registration of equipment, ✉ Resource Management, 1301 Constitution Ave. NW, Washington, DC 20229, ☎ 202/927–0540).

ENTERING CANADA

If you've been out of Canada for at least seven days you may bring in C$500 worth of goods duty-free. If you've been away for fewer than seven days but more than 48 hours, the duty-free allowance drops to C$200; if your trip lasts 24–48 hours, the allowance is C$50. You may not pool allowances with family members. Goods claimed under the C$500 exemption may follow you by mail; those claimed under the lesser exemptions must accompany you.

Alcohol and tobacco products may be included in the seven-day and 48-hour exemptions but not in the 24-hour exemption. If you meet the age requirements of the province or territory through which you reenter Canada you may bring in, duty-free, 1.14 liters (40 imperial ounces) of wine or liquor *or* 24 12-ounce cans or bottles of beer or ale. If you are 16 or older you may bring in, duty-free, 200 cigarettes and 50 cigars; these items must accompany you.

You may send an unlimited number of gifts worth up to C$60 each duty-free to Canada. Label the package UNSOLICITED GIFT—VALUE UNDER $60. Alcohol and tobacco are excluded.

INFORMATION➤ **Revenue Canada** (✉ 2265 St. Laurent Blvd. S, Ottawa, Ontario K1G 4K3, ☎ 613/993–0534, 800/461–9999 in Canada).

ENTERING THE U.K.

From countries outside the EU, including Barbados, you may import, duty-free, 200 cigarettes or 50 cigars; 1 liter of spirits or 2 liters of fortified or sparkling wine or liqueurs; 2 liters of still table wine; 60 milliliters of perfume; 250 milliliters of toilet water; plus £136 worth of other goods, including gifts and souvenirs.

INFORMATION➤ **HM Customs and Excise** (✉ Dorset House, Stamford St., London SE1 9NG, ☎ 0171/202–4227).

ELECTRICITY

The electricity on Barbados is 110 volts, 50 cyles, which is compatible with American appliances. If necessary for your appliances, **bring a converter and an adapter,** although most hotels can provide adapters and transformers.

If your appliances are dual-voltage, you'll need only an adapter. Don't use 110-volt outlets, marked FOR SHAVERS ONLY, for high-wattage appliances such as blow-dryers. Most laptops operate equally well on 110 and 220 volts and so require only an adapter.

EMERGENCIES

CONTACTS➤ **Emergency and Police** (☎ 112). **Ambulance** (☎ 115). **Fire** (☎ 113). **Hospitals:** Queen Elizabeth Hospital (✉ Martindales Rd., St. Michael, ☎ 246/436–6450), Bayview Hospital (private; ✉ St. Paul's Ave., Bayville, St. Michael, ☎ 246/436–5446). **Scuba-diving accidents:** Divers' Alert Network (DAN), (☎ 246/684–8111 or 246/684–2948). **24-hour decompression chamber** (✉ Coast Guard Defence Force, St. Ann's Fort, Garrison, St. Michael, ☎ 246/436–6185).

HEALTH

Insects aren't much of a problem on Barbados, but if you plan to hike or spend time on secluded beaches, it's wise to **use insect repellent.**

The little green apples that fall from the large branches of the manchineel tree may look tempting, but **do not eat or handle them: They are poisonous, and toxic to the touch.** Even taking shelter under the tree when it rains can give you blisters. Most manchineels are identified with signs. If you do come in contact with one, go to the nearest hotel and have someone there phone for a physician.

Sunburn or sunstroke can be serious. A long-sleeve shirt, a hat, and long pants or a beach wrap are essential on a boat, for midday at the beach, and whenever you go out sightseeing. **Use sunblock lotion** on nose, ears, and other sensitive areas, **limit your sun time** for the first few days, and be sure to **drink enough liquids.**

The water on the island is plentiful and safe to drink in hotels and restaurants. It is naturally filtered through 1,000 ft of pervious coral.

DIVERS' ALERT
Do not fly within 24 hours of scuba diving.

HOURS

Bridgetown **stores** are open weekdays 9–5, Saturday 8–1. Out-of-town locations may stay open later. Some supermarkets are open daily 8–6 or later. **Banks** are open Monday–Thursday 8–3, Friday 8–5; at the airport, the Barbados National Bank is open from 8 AM until the last plane leaves or arrives, seven days a week (including holidays).

INSURANCE

Travel insurance is the best way to **protect yourself against financial loss.** The most useful policies are trip-cancellation-and-interruption, default, medical, and comprehensive insurance.

Without insurance you will lose all or most of your money if you cancel your trip, regardless of the reason. It's essential that you **buy trip-cancellation-and-interruption insurance,** particularly if your airline ticket, cruise, or package tour is nonrefundable and cannot be changed. When considering how much coverage you need, look for a policy that will cover the cost of your trip plus the nondiscounted price of a one-way airline ticket, should you need to return home early. Also **consider default or bankruptcy insurance,** which protects you against a supplier's failure to deliver.

Medicare generally does not cover health-care costs outside the United States, nor do many privately issued policies. If your own policy does not cover you outside the United States, **consider buying supplemental medical coverage.** Remember that travel health insurance is different from a medical-assistance plan.

Citizens of the United Kingdom can buy an annual travel-insurance policy valid for most vacations during the year in which it's purchased. If you are pregnant or have a preexisting medical condition, make sure you're covered.

If you have purchased an expensive vacation, comprehensive insurance is a must. Do **look for comprehensive policies that include trip-delay insurance,** which will protect you in the event that weather problems cause you to miss your flight, tour, or cruise. A few insurers sell waivers for preexisting medical conditions. Companies that offer both features include Access America, Carefree Travel, Travel Insured International, and Travel Guard (☞ *below*).

Always **buy travel insurance directly from the insurance company**; if you buy it from a travel agency or tour operator that goes out of business you probably will not be covered for the agency or operator's default, a major risk. Before you make any purchase, **review your existing health and home-owner's policies** to find out whether they cover expenses incurred while traveling.

TRAVEL INSURERS➤ In the U.S.: **Access America** (☒ 6600 W. Broad St., Richmond, VA 23230, ☎ 804/285–3300 or 800/284–8300), **Carefree Travel Insurance** (☒ Box 9366, 100 Garden City Plaza, Garden City, NY 11530, ☎ 516/294–0220 or 800/323–3149), **Near Travel Services** (☒ Box 1339, Calumet City, IL 60409, ☎ 708/868–6700 or 800/654–6700), **Travel Guard International** (☒ 1145 Clark St., Stevens Point, WI 54481, ☎ 715/345–0505 or 800/826–1300), **Travel Insured International** (☒ Box 280568, East Hartford, CT 06128–0568, ☎ 860/528–7663 or 800/243–3174), **Travelex Insurance Services** (☒ 11717 Burt St., Suite 202, Omaha, NE 68154-1500, ☎ 402/445–8637 or 800/228–9792,

FAX 800/867–9531), **Wallach & Company** (⊠ 107 W. Federal St., Box 480, Middleburg, VA 20118, ☎ 540/687–3166 or 800/237–6615). In Canada: **Mutual of Omaha** (⊠ Travel Division, 500 University Ave., Toronto, Ontario M5G 1V8, ☎ 416/598–4083, 800/268–8825 in Canada). In the U.K.: **Association of British Insurers** (⊠ 51 Gresham St., London EC2V 7HQ, ☎ 0171/600–3333).

LANGUAGE

English is spoken everywhere. Some words spoken in the Bajan dialect have an almost Irish lilt.

LODGING

Villa Rentals➤ **Unusual Villas & Island Rentals** (⊠ 101 Tempsford La., Penthouse 9, Richmond, VA 23226, ☎ FAX 804/288–2823). **Villas International** (⊠ 605 Market St., San Francisco, CA 94105, ☎ 415/281–0910 or 800/221–2260, FAX 415/281–0919).

MAIL

An airmail letter from Barbados to the United States or Canada costs Bds90¢ per ½ ounce; an airmail postcard costs Bds65¢. Letters to the United Kingdom are Bds$1.10; postcards are Bds70¢. The main post office, in Cheapside, Bridgetown, is open weekdays 7:30–5; branches in each parish are open weekdays 8–3:15.

MONEY

The Barbados dollar (Bds$1) is tied to the U.S. dollar at the rate of Bds$2 to US$1. Both currencies are accepted island-wide. Prices quoted throughout this chapter are in U.S. dollars unless noted otherwise.

ATMS

Before leaving home, **make sure that your credit cards have been programmed for ATM use in Barbados.** Note that Discover is accepted mostly in the United States. Local bank cards often do not work overseas or may access only your checking account; ask your bank about a MasterCard/Cirrus or Visa debit card, which works like a bank card but can be used at any ATM displaying a MasterCard/Cirrus or Visa logo. These cards, too, may tap only your checking account; check with your bank about their policy.

ATM Locations➤ **Cirrus** (☎ 800/424–7787). A list of **Plus** locations is available at your local bank.

CURRENCY EXCHANGE

For the most favorable rates, **change money at banks.** Although fees charged for ATM transactions may be higher abroad than at home, Cirrus and Plus exchange rates are excellent, because they are based on wholesale rates offered only by major banks. You won't do as well at exchange booths in airports or rail and bus stations, in hotels, in restaurants, or in stores, although you may find their hours more convenient.

To avoid lines at airport exchange booths, **get a small amount of local currency before you leave home.**

EXCHANGE SERVICES➤ **International Currency Express** (☎ 888/842–0880 on the East Coast or 888/278–6628 on the West Coast for telephone orders). **Thomas Cook Currency Services** (☎ 800/287–7362 for telephone orders and retail locations).

TRAVELER'S CHECKS

Whether or not to buy traveler's checks depends on where you are headed—**take cash to rural areas** and small towns, traveler's checks to large towns. If your checks are lost or stolen, they can usually be replaced within 24 hours. To ensure a speedy refund, buy your checks yourself (don't ask someone else to make the purchase). When making a claim for stolen or lost checks, the person who bought the checks should make the call.

PASSPORTS & VISAS

To enter Barbados, U.S. and Canadian citizens need proof of citizenship and a return or ongoing ticket. Acceptable proof of citizenship is a valid passport or an original birth certificate and a photo ID; a voter registration card or baptismal certificate is not acceptable. British citizens need a valid passport.

Once your travel plans are confirmed, **check the expiration date of your passport.** It's also a good idea to **make photocopies of the data page;** leave one copy with someone at home and keep another with you, separated from your passport. If you lose your passport, promptly call the nearest embassy or consulate and the local police; having a copy of the data page can speed replacement.

INFORMATION➤ **Office of Passport Services** (☎ 202/647–0518).

INFORMATION IN CANADA➤ **Passport Office** (☎ 819/994–3500 or 800/567–6868).

INFORMATION IN THE U.K.➤ **London Passport Office** (☎ 0990/21010) for fees and documentation requirements and to request an emergency passport.

TAXES AND SERVICE CHARGES

At the airport you must pay a departure tax of Bds$25 (about US$12.50) in either currency before leaving Barbados; there is no charge for children 12 and under. A 7½% government tax is added to hotel bills; a 10% service charge is added to hotel bills and to most restaurant checks. Any additional tip recognizes extraordinary service. When no service charge is added, tip maids $1 per room per day, waiters 10%–15%, taxi drivers 10%. Airport porters and bellboys expect 50¢–$1 per bag.

TAXIS

Taxis operate at a fixed hourly rate of Bds$35 for up to 3 passengers. For short trips, the rate per mile (or part thereof) should not exceed Bds$3. Before you start off, **settle the rate and agree on whether it's in U.S. or Barbados dollars.** Most drivers will gladly narrate a tour.

TELEPHONES

The area code for Barbados is 246. Except for emergency numbers (☞ Emergencies, *above*) all phone numbers have seven digits and begin with 22, 23, 42, or 43.

CALLING HOME

Before you go, **find out the local access codes** for your destinations. AT&T, MCI, and Sprint long-distance services make calling home relatively convenient, but you may find the local access number blocked in many hotel rooms. First ask the hotel operator to connect you. If the hotel operator balks, ask for an international operator, or dial the international operator yourself. One way to improve your odds of getting connected to your long-distance carrier is to travel with more than one company's calling card (a hotel may block Sprint, for example, but not MCI). If all else fails, call your phone company collect in the United States or call from a pay phone in the hotel lobby.

To OBTAIN ACCESS CODES➤ **AT&T USADirect** (☎ 800/874–4000). **MCI Call USA** (☎ 800/444–4444). **Sprint Express** (☎ 800/793–1153).

TOUR OPERATORS

Buying a prepackaged tour or independent vacation can make your trip to Barbados less expensive and more hassle-free. Because everything is prearranged you'll spend less time planning.

Operators that handle several hundred thousand travelers per year can use their purchasing power to give you a good price. Their high volume may also indicate financial stability. But some small companies provide more personalized service; because they tend to specialize, they may also be more knowledgeable about a given area.

A GOOD DEAL?

The more your package or tour includes, the better you can predict the ultimate cost of your vacation. Make sure you know exactly what is covered, and **beware of hidden costs.** Are taxes, tips, and service charges included? Transfers and baggage handling? Entertainment and excursions? These can add up.

If the package or tour you are considering is priced lower than in your wildest dreams, **be skeptical.** Also, **make sure your travel agent knows the accommodations** and other services. Ask about the hotel's location, room size, beds, and whether it has a pool, room service, or programs for children, if you care about these. Has your agent been there in person or sent others you can contact?

BUYER BEWARE

Each year consumers are stranded or lose their money when tour operators—even very large ones with excellent reputations—go out of business. So **check out the operator.** Find out how long the company has been in business, and ask several agents about its reputation. **Don't book unless the firm has a consumer-protection program.**

Members of the National Tour Association and United States Tour Operators Association are required to set aside funds to cover your payments and travel arrangements in case the company defaults. Nonmembers may carry insurance instead. Look for the details, and for the name of an underwriter with a solid reputation, in the operator's brochure. Note: When it comes to tour operators, **don't trust escrow accounts.** Although the Department of Transportation watches over charter-flight operators, no regulatory body prevents tour operators from raiding the till. You may want to protect yourself by buying travel insurance that includes a tour-operator default provision.

It's also a good idea to choose a company that participates in the American Society of Travel Agent's Tour Operator Program (TOP). This gives you a forum if there are any disputes between you and

your tour operator; ASTA will act as mediator.

TOUR-OPERATOR RECOMMENDA-TIONS➤ **National Tour Association** (NTA; ⊠ 546 E. Main St., Lexington, KY 40508, ☎ 606/226–4444 or 800/755–8687). **United States Tour Operators Association** (USTOA; ⊠ 342 Madison Ave., Suite 1522, New York, NY 10173, ☎ 212/599–6599, FAX 212/599–6744). **American Society of Travel Agents** (☞ *below*).

AGENTS

Travel agents are excellent resources. In fact, large operators accept bookings made only through travel agents. But it's a good idea to **collect brochures from several agencies,** because some agents' suggestions may be influenced by relationships with tour and package firms that reward them for volume sales. If you have a special interest, **find an agent with expertise in that area;** ASTA (☞ Travel Agencies, *below*) has a database of specialists worldwide. Do some homework on your own, too: Local tourism boards can provide information about lesser-known and small-niche operators, some of which may sell only direct.

SINGLE TRAVELERS

Prices for packages and tours are usually quoted per person, based on two sharing a room. If traveling solo, you may be required to pay the full double-occupancy rate. Some operators eliminate this surcharge if you agree to be matched with a roommate of the same sex, even if one is not found by departure time.

GUIDED TOURS

For half- and full-day tour operators in Barbados, *see* Chapter 7.

PACKAGES

Independent vacation packages are available from major tour operators and airlines. The companies listed below offer vacation packages in a broad price range.

AIR/HOTEL➤ **American Airlines Fly AAway Vacations** (☎ 800/321–2121). **Certified Vacations** (✉ 110 E. Broward Blvd., Fort Lauderdale, FL 33302, ☎ 954/522–1440 or 800/233–7260). **Delta Dream Vacations** (☎ 800/872–7786, FAX 954/357–4687).

TRAVEL AGENCIES

A good travel agent puts your needs first. Look for an agency that has been in business at least five years, emphasizes customer service, and has someone on staff who specializes in your destination. In addition, **make sure the agency belongs to the American Society of Travel Agents** (ASTA). If your travel agency is also acting as your tour operator, *see* Tour Operators, *above*.

LOCAL AGENT REFERRALS➤ **American Society of Travel Agents** (ASTA, ☎ 800/965–2782, 24-hr hot line, FAX 703/684–8319). Al-

liance of Canadian Travel Associations (✉ Suite 201, 1729 Bank St., Ottawa, Ontario K1V 7Z5, ☎ 613/521–0474, FAX 613/521–0805). **Association of British Travel Agents** (✉ 55–57 Newman St., London W1P 4AH, ☎ 0171/637–2444, FAX 0171/637–0713).

VISITOR INFORMATION

The **Barbados Tourist Authority** can be a good source of general information, up-to-date calendars of events, and listings of hotels, restaurants, sights, and shops.

IN THE U.S.➤ ✉ 800 2nd Ave., 2nd floor, New York, NY 10017, ☎ 212/986–6516 or 800/221–9831, FAX 212/573–9850; ✉ 2442 Hinge St., Troy, MI 48083, ☎ 810/740–7835, FAX 810/740–9434; ✉ 3440 Wilshire Blvd., Suite 1215, Los Angeles, CA 90010, ☎ 213/380–2198, FAX 213/384–2763.

IN CANADA➤ ✉ 5160 Yonge St., Suite 1800, N. York, Ontario M2N–6L9, ☎ 416/512–6569 or 800/268–9122, FAX 416/512–6581.

IN THE U.K.➤ ✉ 263 Tottenham Court Rd., London W1P 0LA, ☎ 0171/636–9448, FAX 0171/637–1496.

IN BARBADOS➤ The **Barbados Tourism Authority** is on Harbour Road in Bridgetown (☎ 246/427–2623, FAX 246/426–4080). Hours are 8:30–4:30 weekdays. Information booths, staffed by Tourism Authority representatives, are at

Grantley Adams International Airport (☎ 246/428–0937) and at Bridgetown's Cruise Ship Terminal (☎ 246/426–1718).

WHEN TO GO

The Caribbean high season is traditionally winter, usually extending from December 15 to April 14. This is when northern weather is at its worst, not necessarily when Caribbean weather is at its best. In fact, winter is when the Caribbean is at its windiest. It's also the most fashionable, the most expensive, and the most popular time to visit, and most hotels are heavily booked. You have to make your reservations at least two or three months in advance for the very best places. Hotel prices drop 20%–50% for summer (after April 15); cruise prices also fall.

CLIMATE

It's hot and sunny all year in Barbados, with an average daytime high of 85°F. Northeast trade winds keep it from becoming unbearably hot, and nights cool down to around 77°F.

As part of the fall's rainy season, hurricanes occasionally sweep through the Caribbean. Check the news daily, and keep abreast of brewing tropical storms by reading Stateside papers if you can get them. The rainy season consists mostly of brief showers interspersed with sunshine. You can watch the clouds come over, feel the rain, and remain on your lounge chair for the sun to dry you off. A spell of overcast days is "unusual," as everyone will tell you.

FORECASTS➤ **Weather Channel Connection** (☎ 900/932–8437), 95¢ per minute from a Touch-Tone phone.

1 Destination: Barbados

BARBADOS—BRITISH TO ITS CARIBBEAN CORE

BARBADOS HAS A LIFE of its own that continues after the tourists have packed up their sun oils and returned home. The government is stable, business operations are sophisticated, literacy is over 95%, and unemployment is relatively low, so the difference between haves and have-nots is less marked—or at least less visible—than on some islands. A United Nations Development Index ranking in 1996 put Barbados third behind Hong Kong and Cyprus in terms of quality of life, ranking it ahead of countries such as Spain and Italy. The 260,000 Bajans (Barbadians) are warm, friendly, and hospitable people. They are genuinely proud of their country and welcome visitors as privileged guests.

Barbados sits at the most easterly point of all the Caribbean islands, partially in the Atlantic Ocean and partially in the Caribbean Sea. It is 21 mi long, 14 mi wide, and relatively flat, although the highest point, Mt. Hillaby, has an elevation of 1,115 ft. Most people live between Speightstown, on the northwest coast, and Oistins, in the south, the urban area surrounding Bridgetown, the capital. Others reside in tiny hamlets scattered around the island.

Beaches along the tranquil West Coast—in the lee of the northwest trade winds—are backed by first-class resorts. Additional hotels stretch along the beaches on the South Coast, where Americans (couples more often than singles) tend to congregate. British and Canadian visitors often favor the posh hotels in the parish of St. James. As on the other islands in the Caribbean, the beaches of Barbados are open to the public; all are lovely, with white sand, and many are secluded.

Toward the northeast are rolling hills and valleys covered by impenetrable acres of sugarcane. Sugar—"white gold"—exports led to great wealth and stature for the island beginning in the late 1600s. In 1846, almost 500 plantations covered the island; today, 1,500 small farms, without the benefit of mechanization, can produce 60,000 tons of sugar each year—given no cane fires or droughts. The high point of the year, the summertime Crop-Over Festival, marks the end of the labor-intensive harvest.

The Atlantic surf pounds against gigantic boulders along the rugged east coast, where the Bajans themselves have vacation homes. Elsewhere on the island, crisscrossed by almost 900 mi of good roads, are small villages, historic plantation houses, stalactite-studded caves, a wildlife preserve, and the Andromeda Gardens, one of the most attractive small tropical gardens in the world.

No one is sure whether the name Los Barbados ("the bearded ones") refers to the beardlike root that hangs from the island's fig trees, to the bearded natives who greeted the Portuguese "discoverer" of the island in 1536, or to any other theory surrounding the appellation. The name Los Barbados was being used almost a century later when the British landed—by accident—in what is now Holetown, in the parish of St. James. They colonized the island in 1627, and British rule remained uninterrupted until the island achieved independence in 1966.

Barbados retains a very British atmosphere. Afternoon tea is a ritual at numerous hotels. Cricket, the national sport, is also the national passion—Barbados produces some of the world's top players. Polo, "the sport of kings," is played all winter. The British tradition of dressing for dinner is firmly entrenched, yet the island's atmosphere is hardly stuffy. This is still the Caribbean, after all.

FESTIVALS AND SEASONAL EVENTS

In mid-January, the **Barbados Windsurfing World Championship** (☎ 246/426–5837) takes place on the southeast coast of the island, one of the top three windsurfing locations in the world. Also in mid-January, the **Barbados Jazz Festival** in Bridgetown features performances of original compositions and traditional jazz for three days. The **Barbados National Trust** (☎ 246/436–9033) conducts tours of private homes of architectural or historical interest one afternoon each week between January and April.

Barbados's **Holetown Festival** commemorates the first settlement of Barbados (February 17, 1627), with a week of fairs, street markets, the Royal Police Band Concert, and revelry. **Holder's Opera Season** in March features Shakespeare plays and the likes of Luciano Pavarotti (☎ 246/432–6345).

For more than 20 years Bajans have celebrated at the **Oistins Fish Festival** from late March to early April to honor the local fishing industry and the gifts of the sea. Besides the food stalls, crafts displays, calypso and reggae music, and dancing, there are fish boning and grease-pole competitions.

The Congaline Village hosts the **De Congaline Street Festival** at the end of April through the first week of May. This nine-day carnival includes free entertainment, crafts, and culture. The **Gospelfest** in May attracts Gospel choirs from the U.S., the U.K., and the Caribbean.

Beginning in late June and continuing through August, Bajans celebrate the **Crop-Over Festival,** a monthlong cheer for the end of the sugarcane harvest—their equivalent to other islands' carnivals. Calypsonians battle for the coveted Calypso Monarch award,

and Bajan cooking abounds at the massive Bridgetown Market street fair.

At the **Caribbean Story-Telling Festival** in July, story-tellers from around the Caribbean spin their tales in public forums, tents, and schools.

National holidays include **Errol Barrow Day,** in honor of the former Prime Minister, on January 21; the last day of the Crop-Over Festival, **Kadooment Day,** on August 4; and **Independence Day** (realized from Great Britain in 1966) on November 30.

2 Lodging

THE SOUTHERN AND WESTERN shores of Barbados are lined with hotels and resorts of every size and price, offering accommodations ranging from private villas and elegant hotels to modest but comfortable rooms in simple inns. Apartment and home rentals and time-share condominiums have become widely available and are growing increasingly popular. Most of the hotels run on the EP meal plan but also offer CP or MAP; a few are all-inclusive.

The location of your hotel is important. Hotels to the north of Bridgetown, in the West Coast parishes of St. Peter, St. James, and St. Michael, tend to be self-contained resorts with stretches of empty road between them that discourage strolling to a neighborhood bar or restaurant. Along the South Coast, in Christ Church, many of the hotels cluster near or along the busy strip known as St. Lawrence Gap, where dozens of small restaurants, bars, and nightclubs are close by. Hotels listed here are grouped by parish.

CATEGORY	COST*
$$$$	over $350
$$$	$250–$350
$$	$150–$250
$	under $150

All prices are for a standard double room, excluding 7½% government tax and 10% service charge.

Hotels and Resorts

St. James

$$$$ 🏨 **Coral Reef Club.** Guests here spend their days relaxing on the white-sand beach or around the pool, taking time out for the hotel's superb afternoon tea. The public areas ramble along the beach and face the Caribbean Sea, and small coral-stone cottages are scattered over the surrounding 12 flower-filled acres. (The cottages farthest from the beach are a bit of a hike to the main house.) The rooms are spacious, each with air-conditioning and ceiling fans, a small patio, and fresh flowers. The restaurant, under the direction of Bajan chef Graham Licorish, is noted for its inventive cuisine, which combines local cooking with European flair. Most guests are on a MAP. Another convenience is the free shuttle into Bridgetown. ⊠ *Porters,* ☎ *246/422–2372,* FAX *246/422–1776. 68 rooms. Restaurant, air-conditioning, fans, pool, beach, snorkeling, windsurfing, waterskiing. AE, MC, V. EP, MAP.*

$$$$ 🏨 **Glitter Bay.** In the 1930s, Sir Edward Cunard, of the English shipping family, bought this estate, built a Great House and a beach house that resembled his palazzo in Venice. Cunard's parties in honor of visiting aristocrats and celebrities gave Glitter Bay an early reputation for grandeur and style. Today, newer buildings angled back from the beach contain 70 one- to three-bedroom suites, some with full kitchens; the beach house is now five garden suites. Manicured gardens separate the reception area and a large, comfortable tea lounge from an alfresco dining room (where evening entertainment is held), the pool, and a half mile of beach. Glitter Bay is more casual and family-oriented than its next-door sister property, the Royal Pavilion (☞ *below*), but the resorts share facilities, including complimentary water sports, and dining privileges. ⊠ *Porters,* ☎ *246/422–5555,* FAX *246/ 422–3940. 83 rooms. Restaurant, air-conditioning, pool, beauty salon, health club, golf privileges, 2 tennis courts, beach, water sports. AE, DC, MC, V. EP, MAP.*

$$$$ 🏨 **Royal Pavilion.** Of the 75 rooms here, 72 are ocean-
★ front suites; the remaining three are nestled in a garden villa. The ground-floor rooms allow guests simply to step through sliding doors, cross their private patio, and walk onto the sand. Second- and third-floor rooms have the advantage of an elevated view of the sea. Breakfast and lunch are served alfresco along the edge of the beach. Afternoon tea and dinner are in the Palm Terrace (☞ Chapter 3). The Royal Pavilion attracts sophisticated guests who want serenity (bringing children under the age of 12 is discouraged during the winter months). Recreational facilities and dining privileges are shared with the adjoining and more informal sister hotel, Glitter Bay (☞ *above*). ⊠ *Porters,* ☎ *246/422– 5555,* FAX *246/422–3940. 75 rooms. 2 restaurants, 2 bars,*

8

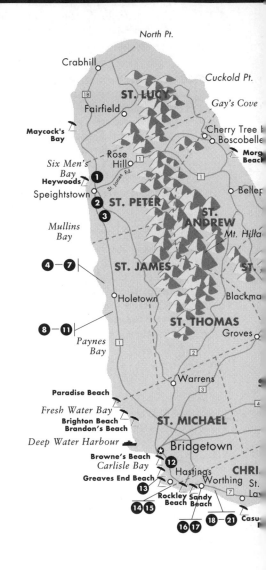

Lodging

0   3 miles

0   3 km

Pt.

'ove

ree Hill
belle

Morgan Lewis
Beach

elleplaine

lillaby   *Tent Bay*

25 **26**

Bathsheba

T. JOSEPH   *Consett*
                       Bay

mans

Four   *Ragged*
Crossroads   Marley   *Pt.*
          ST. JOHN   Vale

                            Bottom
                            Bay

Gun Hill

          4

          4B

ST. GEORGE   **ST. PHILIP**   **24**

4   Edgecumbe

                    The Crane   **Crane Beach**
                            23
                            Crane
                            Bay
                    Foul Bay

                       COBBLER'S REEF

RIST CHURCH

St.
Lawrence   **Grantley Adams**
          7   **International**
                    Airport
22 Oistins   *Long*
                    Bay
suarina
Beach
          Oistins   **Silver Sands Beach**
          Bay
          South Pt.

A T L A N T I C   O C E A N

N

*air-conditioning, pool, beauty salon, golf privileges, 2
tennis courts, beach, water sports. AE, DC, MC, V. EP.*

$$$$ ⊞ **Sandy Lane Hotel.** This prestigious hotel has set a
★ standard for elegance and style since 1961. On one of
the best beaches in Barbados, with acres of well-tended
grounds, Sandy Lane is one of the most impressive hotels in the Caribbean. The white coral structure, with
marble throughout has a grand staircase leading to the
best beach on the West Coast. The scene, the style, and
the atmosphere are reminiscent of *The Great Gatsby.*
All rooms overlook the sea and have private balconies
for eating breakfast and watching magnificent sunsets.
Rooms are nothing short of spectacular; bathrooms are
vast and luxurious. Afternoon tea, fine dining, and personalized service all add to the charm. You'll be treated
like royalty—in fact, royalty does stay here. Plan to
dress up, particularly in season—no jeans or shorts after
7 PM. ⊠ *Hwy. 1,* ☎ *246/432–1311,* 𝔽𝔸𝕏 *246/432–2954.
90 rooms, 30 suites. 3 restaurants, 5 bars, air-conditioning, pool, beauty salon, health club, 18-hole golf
course, 5 tennis courts, beach, water sports, baby-sitting, children's programs. AE, DC, MC, V. EP, MAP.*

$$$ ⊞ **Coconut Creek Club.** The atmosphere is casual at
this luxury cottage colony, set on handsomely land-
scaped grounds with a small private beach and a bar
pavilion for entertainment and dancing. From a low bluff,
the hotel overlooks the ocean, and steps lead down to
two secluded coves. Some rooms have ocean views; oth-
ers overlook the garden or pool. Televisions are avail-
able on request for a small fee. ⊠ *Reservations: Box 249,
Bridgetown; Hwy. 1,* ☎ *246/432–0803,* 𝔽𝔸𝕏 *246/432–
0272. 53 rooms. Bar, dining room, air-conditioning, pool,
beach, water sports, baby-sitting. AE, DC, MC, V. EP,
MAP.*

$$$ ⊞ **Discovery Bay Hotel.** In historic Holetown, site of the
British "discovery" and settlement of the island, this quiet
hotel—with a grand, white-columned, plantation-style
entrance—is surrounded by 4½ acres of tropical gardens
and bordered by a broad strand of Caribbean beach.
Deluxe rooms have ocean views; others open onto a central lawn and pool area. A shuttle to Bridgetown is

available to guests on weekdays. ⊠ *Hwy. 1, Holetown,* ☎ *246/432–1301,* FAX *246/432–2553. 87 rooms. Restaurant, air-conditioning, pool, Ping-Pong, beach, shop. AE, D, DC, MC, V. EP.*

$$$ ⛉ **Treasure Beach.** Most of the one-bedroom suites of this compact resort create a horseshoe around a small garden and pool, other suites have sea views, but all are just steps from the beach. Suites are spacious, with kitchenettes and sitting rooms that open onto large patios or verandas with louvered, full-length shutters for privacy. The restaurant's reputation for gourmet dining and fine service attracts an outside clientele as well as hotel guests. The atmosphere here is quiet and pleasant. Guests, particularly British vacationers, often stay two or three weeks, giving the hotel an almost residential quality. ⊠ *Paynes Bay,* ☎ *246/432–1346,* FAX *246/432–1094. 24 1-bedroom suites, 1 2-bedroom penthouse suite. Restaurant, air-conditioning, pool, beach, water sports. AE, DC, MC, V. EP, MAP.*

$$–$$$ ⛉ **Almond Beach Club.** In this hotel, everything is included in the price of the room—all you want to eat and drink (including wine and liquor), water sports, boat trips, tennis, a Bajan beach picnic, shopping excursions to Bridgetown, departure transportation to the airport, and service and taxes. Accommodations are in one-bedroom suites with balconies, two-bedroom duplex suites, and individual poolside or garden-view rooms. The food is excellent, from the breakfast buffet and four-course lunch to the afternoon tea and pastries and the intimate, candlelit service at dinner. If your stay is seven days or more, you can choose the dine-around program—dinner or lunch at area restaurants with round-trip transportation included. The exchange program with Almond Beach Village (☞ *below*) includes golf privileges; shuttle service is provided. The Almond Beach Club doesn't have the enforced-activity, "whistle-blowing" atmosphere of some other all-inclusives. ⊠ *Vauxhall,* ☎ *246/432–7840 or 800/425–6663,* FAX *246/432–2115. 161 rooms. 2 restaurants, 4 bars, air-conditioning, 3 pools, sauna, tennis court, squash, beach, water sports, shop. AE, MC, V. All-inclusive.*

St. Peter

$$$$ ⊞ **Cobblers Cove Hotel.** This all-suite resort, 12 mi up
★ the West Coast from Bridgetown, combines comfort
and informal elegance in an English-style country house.
The pink-and-white building and the tropical gardens
are bordered on three sides by stone walls, giving the
property a self-contained ambience. This fine retreat overlooking the sea and small beach is the only member of
the Relais & Châteaux organization in Barbados. There's
an excellent gourmet restaurant and a clublike lounge-
library, and the bar becomes the evening gathering spot.
For all-out luxury, stay in the new Colleton Suite or the
Camelot Suite. Guests enjoy special rates and guaran-
teed tee times at the nearby Royal Westmoreland Golf
Course. No children under 12 are allowed from late January to late March. ⊠ *Hwy. 1,* ☎ *246/422–2291 or
800/890–6060,* ℻ *246/422–1460. 40 suites. Restaurant, bar, snack bar, air-conditioning, pool, tennis, water
sports, baby-sitting. AE, MC, V. CP, MAP.*

$$$ ⊞ **Almond Beach Village.** The sister hotel to the Almond
★ Beach Club (☞ *above*) in St. James, this is a spacious
30-acre resort on a mile of beachfront, with an execu-
tive, three-par golf course (clubs provided), nine pools,
a full range of land and water sports, and other guest
activities (shopping excursions to Bridgetown, island
tours, a Bajan picnic off-property, a Caribbean cook-
ing school, and a dine-around program). A shuttle be-
tween the Village and the Club allows guests to use
both resorts' facilities. Guest rooms, in seven low-rise
buildings, are spacious, comfortable, and attractively dec-
orated. A family section has junior and one-bedroom
suites, a nursery, a play area, a wading pool, and a su-
pervised Kid's Klub. An historic sugar mill on the prop-
erty is a lovely spot for wedding ceremonies. The
restaurants serve Continental, Italian, and native cuisine.
All meals (including beverages), activities, and depar-
ture transfers are included in the rates. ⊠ *Hwy. 1,* ☎
246/422–4900 or 800/425–6663, ℻ *246/422–1581.
288 rooms. 4 restaurants, 5 bars, air-conditioning, 9
pools, wading pool, 9-hole golf course, 5 tennis courts,
exercise room, squash, beach, water sports, shop, dance
club. AE, MC, V. All-inclusive.*

$$ 🏨 **Sandridge.** Six new waterfront suites and a new dining room with lounge have been added to this fashionable beachfront property near Speightstown. Guest rooms have been restyled in bright colors with tropical furnishings; some rooms have kitchenettes. Ground-floor accommodations have wide doors and ramps, allowing easy access for guests with disabilities. A supervised children's program makes this property particularly attractive to families. The resort's second pool has been remodeled to include a dramatic waterfall and deck of coral stone. ⊠ *Road View,* ☎ *246/422–2361,* ⒻⒶⓍ *246/422–1965. 58 rooms. 2 restaurants, 2 bars, air-conditioning, 2 pools, beach, water sports, baby-sitting. AE, DC, MC, V. EP.*

St. Michael

$$–$$$ 🏨 **Barbados Hilton.** This large resort, just five minutes from Bridgetown, bustles with activity from the people who come to attend seminars and conferences. An atrium lobby greets you when you arrive, and there's a 1,000-ft-wide man-made beach with full water sports and lots of shops to keep you busy. All rooms and suites have balconies. ⊠ *Needham's Point,* ☎ *246/426–0200,* ⒻⒶⓍ *246/436–8946. 184 rooms. Restaurant, 2 bars, lobby lounge, air-conditioning, pool, 4 tennis courts, health club, beach. AE, DC, MC, V. EP.*

$$ 🏨 **Grand Barbados Beach Resort.** A mile south of Bridgetown on Carlisle Bay, this convenient hotel has comfortable rooms and suites. The white-sand beach is lapped by a surprisingly clear sea despite the oil refinery nearby. The Aquatic Club executive floor has rooms whose rates include a Continental breakfast and secretarial services. Nightly live music, a dance floor, and a 260-ft-long pier that's perfect for romantic walks add to the enjoyment of a stay here. ⊠ *Box 639, Bridgetown,* ☎ *246/426–4000,* ⒻⒶⓍ *246/429–2400. 133 rooms. 2 restaurants, air-conditioning, pool, barbershop, beauty salon, hot tub, sauna, tennis court, exercise room, beach, shops. AE, DC, MC, V. EP.*

Christ Church

$$ 🏨 **Accra Beach Hotel & Resort.** Totally renovated in 1996, the four-story Accra reopened with beautifully appointed

rooms and suites, each with a balcony facing the sandy white beach. Rooms are attractively decorated in soft pastel colors. Six duplex penthouse suites have sitting rooms downstairs and a spacious bedroom and huge bath with whirlpool upstairs. Between the hotel and its beach are a large double pool, snack bar, and poolside bar for drinks. In the evening, after sumptuous dining in the Sirocco restaurant, take a turn on a dance floor that's open to the stars. Children under 12 stay free in their parents' room. ⊠ *Box 73W, Rockley,* ☎ *246/435–8920,* ℻ *246/435–6794. 122 rooms. 3 restaurants, 2 bars, air-conditioning, pool, beauty salon, squash, beach, shops, meeting room. AE, DC, MC, V. EP, MAP.*

$$ ▦ **Casuarina Beach Club.** This luxury apartment hotel consists of five clusters of Spanish-style buildings in 7½ acres of gardens. The hotel takes its name from the casuarina pines that surround it. The quiet setting provides a dramatic contrast to that of other South Coast resorts. The bar and restaurant are on the beach—900 ft of pink sand. A reception area includes small lounges where you can get a dose of TV (there aren't any in the bedrooms). Rooms have kitchenettes and large balconies. Scuba diving, golf, and other activities can be arranged. The Casuarina Beach is popular with those who prefer self-catering holidays in a secluded setting yet want to be close to nightlife and shopping. ⊠ *St. Lawrence Gap,* ☎ *246/428–3600 or 800/223–9815,* ℻ *246/428–1970. 134 rooms. Restaurant, bar, air-conditioning, pool, 2 tennis courts, squash, beach, shop. AE, DC, MC, V. EP.*

$$ ▦ **Club Rockley Barbados.** Some of these time-share condominiums have been transformed into an all-inclusive resort with one- and two-bedroom accommodations with balcony or patio. The remaining time-share condominiums are set apart from the hotel facility. On 65 acres near (but not on) one of the most popular beach areas in Barbados, the resort offers an extensive list of guest amenities and an excellent location for golfers and tennis players. ⊠ *Golf Club Rd., Hastings,* ☎ *246/435–7880,* ℻ *246/435–8015. 288 rooms. 2 restaurants, 3 bars, air-conditioning, 7 pools, beauty salon, 9-hole* *golf course, 5 tennis courts, squash, shops. AE, DC, MC, V. All-inclusive.*

$$ ⊞ **Divi Southwinds Beach Resort.** In this resort, on 20 lush acres, the toss-up is whether to take one of the one-bedroom suites, with a balcony and kitchenette overlooking the gardens and pool, or one of the smaller and older-looking rooms, just steps from the sandy white beach. Though all the rooms are pleasant, the buildings themselves are rather plain. Guests come here for action, and that includes making full use of the scuba and water-sports facilities. ⊠ *St. Lawrence Gap,* ☎ *246/428–7181 or 800/367–3484,* 𝟙𝟙 *246/428–4674. 166 rooms. 2 restaurants, air-conditioning, 3 pools, putting green, 2 tennis courts, beach, water sports, shops. AE, MC, V. EP, MAP.*

$$ ⊞ **Sandy Beach Island Resort.** On a wide, sparkling white beach, this comfortable hotel has a popular poolside bar and the Beachfront Restaurant, which serves a West Indian buffet Tuesday and Saturday nights. The accommodations have been reconfigured and upgraded to include large one-bedroom suites, the restaurant has been enlarged, and a boardwalk gazebo, roof garden, and spectacular free-form pool have been added to the grounds. Scuba-diving certification, deep-sea fishing, harbor cruises, and catamaran sailing can be arranged. It's also a convenient walk to St. Lawrence Gap for restaurants and entertainment. ⊠ *Worthing,* ☎ *246/435–8000,* 𝟙𝟙 *246/435–8053. 89 units. Restaurant, bar, air-conditioning, pool, beach. AE, DC, MC, V. EP.*

$$ ⊞ **Southern Palms.** A plantation-style hotel on a 1,000-ft stretch of pink sand near the Dover Convention Center, this is a convenient businessperson's hotel and a good choice for active guests wanting to be near the Gap's shops and restaurants. You may choose from standard bedrooms, deluxe oceanfront suites with kitchenettes, and a four-bedroom penthouse. Each wing of the hotel has its own small pool. ⊠ *St. Lawrence Gap,* ☎ *246/428–7171,* 𝟙𝟙 *246/428–7175. 93 rooms. 2 restaurants, bar, air-conditioning, 2 pools, miniature golf, tennis court, beach, water sports, shop, convention center. AE, DC, MC, V. EP.*

$ ⛶ **Little Bay Hotel.** This small hotel is a find for any-
one who wants to go easy on the wallet and yet sleep
to the sounds of the sea. Each room has a private balcony, bedroom, small lounge, and kitchenette. Ceiling
fans will keep you cool, but there are no TVs in the
rooms—you can catch up on the news and watch sports
in the small lounge next to the popular restaurant,
Southern Accents. ⊠ *St. Lawrence Gap,* ☎ *246/435–
7246,* ℻ *246/435–8574. 10 rooms. Restaurant, bar,
lounge, beach. AE, MC, V. EP.*

$ ⛶ **Oasis Hotel.** The Oasis (formerly the Sichris Hotel)
is a real find. More attractive inside than it appears from
the road, it's a comfortable and convenient self-contained
hotel. Just minutes from the city, the one-bedroom suites
all have kitchenettes and private balconies or patios. It's
a walk of two or three minutes to the beach. ⊠ *Worthing,* ☎ *246/435–7930,* ℻ *246/435–8232. 24 rooms.
Restaurant, bar, air-conditioning, pool. AE, DC, MC,
V. EP.*

$ ⛶ **Windsurf Village Barbados.** A small hotel that began
as a gathering place for windsurfing enthusiasts, Windsurf Village Barbados (formerly Benston Windsurfing
Club Hotel) is now a complete school and center for the
sport, with plans to expand the facility even more. The
rooms are spacious and sparsely furnished to accommodate the active and young crowd who choose this bare-
bones hotel right on the beach. The bar and restaurant
overlook the water. All sports can be arranged, but
windsurfing (learning, practicing, and perfecting it) is
king. ⊠ *Maxwell Main Rd.,* ☎ *246/428–9095,* ℻ *246/
428–2872. 18 rooms. Restaurant, bar, beach, windsurfing. AE, MC, V. EP.*

St. Philip

$$$ ⛶ **Crane Beach Hotel.** This remote hilltop property on
a cliff overlooking the dramatic Atlantic coast remains
one of the special places of Barbados. The Crane Beach
has suites and one-bedrooms. Rooms are decorated
with four-poster beds and antique furniture; rates vary
depending on the view. Corner suite 1 is one of the
nicest rooms, with its two walls of windows and patio
terrace. The Roman-style pool with columns separates

the main house from the dining room. To reach the beach, you walk down some 200 steps onto a beautiful stretch of sand thumped by waves that are good for both bodysurfing and swimming. ⊠ *Crane Bay,* ☎ *246/ 423–6220,* ﷽ *246/423–5343. 18 rooms. Restaurant, bar, 2 pools, 4 tennis courts, beach. AE, DC, MC, V. EP, MAP.*

$$ ⊡ **Sam Lord's Castle.** Set on the Atlantic coast about 14 mi east of Bridgetown, Sam Lord's Castle is not a castle with moat and towers but a great house surrounded by 72 acres of grounds, gardens, and beach. The seven rooms in the main house have canopied beds; downstairs, the public rooms have furniture by Sheraton, Hepplewhite, and Chippendale—for admiring, not for sitting. Additional guest rooms in surrounding cottages have conventional hotel furnishings. The beach is a mile long, the Wanderer Restaurant offers Continental cuisine, and there are even a few slot machines, as befits a pirate's lair. A special tennis package includes unlimited court time, airport transfers, and a Thursday Shipwreck party. ⊠ *Long Bay,* ☎ *246/423–7350,* ﷽ *246/423–5918. 234 rooms. 3 restaurants, air-conditioning, 3 pools, 7 tennis courts, beach. AE, D, DC, MC, V. EP, MAP.*

St. Joseph

$ ⊡ **Atlantis Hotel.** The Atlantis provides a warm, pleasant atmosphere in a quiet area of the majestically rocky Atlantic coast, where the views out to the open sea are mesmerizing. The hotel is modest, yet the congeniality and the Bajan food more than make up for that. There's a beachfront, but Bathsheba beach is right next door and a safer place to swim and surf. ⊠ *Bathsheba,* ☎ *246/ 433–9445. 8 rooms. Restaurant, bar, beach. AE. EP.*

$ ⊡ **Edgewater Inn.** If you enjoy peace and quiet and want
★ a room with a view, this is the place. The inn is perched on a cliff overlooking the pounding surf and unusual rock formations at Bathsheba Beach. Bounded by Joe's River, a national park, and a 9-mi strip of sand, the property also backs up to an 85-acre rain forest. Yoga classes, nature walks, and guided hikes are available to guests. All rooms have an ocean view and handmade mahogany

furniture. In fact, doors, moldings, and dining-room furniture are also fashioned from hand-hewn local mahogany. A shuttle will meet your plane or take you shopping, snorkeling, or pub crawling. But overall, you must be content with watching the birds and butterflies, taking a hike, or surfing Soup Bowl most of the time. ⊠ *Bathsheba, St. Joseph,* ☎ *246/433–9900,* FAX *246/433–9902. 20 rooms. Restaurant, bar, pool, beach. AE, MC, V. CP.*

Villas and Condominiums

Villas, private homes, and condos are available for rent south of Bridgetown in the Hastings-Worthing area, along the coast of St. James, and in St. Peter. As an example, two- to three-bedroom condos near the beach start at $800–$1,000 per week in the summer months—double that in winter. Most include maid service, and a cook can be arranged through the owner or manager. Rentals are also available through Barbados realtors; among them are **Alleyne, Aguilar & Altman** (⊠ Rosebank, St. James, ☎ 246/432–0840), **Bajan Services** (⊠ St. Peter, ☎ 246/422–2618), and **Ronald Stoute & Sons Ltd.** (⊠ St. Philip, ☎ 246/423–6800). The **Barbados Tourism Authority** (☎ 246/427–2623, FAX 246/426–4080) has a listing of apartments and rates. In the United States, contact **At Home Abroad** (☎ 212/421–9165) or Jan Pizzi at **Villa Vacations** (☎ 617/593–8885 or 800/800–5576).

3 Dining

TO ATTRACT AND KEEP their sophisticated clientele, the better hotels and restaurants of Barbados employ chefs who have been trained in New York and Europe. Gourmet dining here usually includes fresh seafood, beef, or veal with finely blended sauces.

West Indian cuisine offers an entirely different dining experience. The African heritage brings to the table rice, peas, beans, and okra, the staples that make a perfect base for slowly cooked meat and fish dishes. Many side dishes are cooked in oil (the pumpkin fritters can be addictive). And be cautious at first with the West Indian condiments; like the sun, they are hotter than you think.

Some local specialties:

Buljol is a cold salad of marinated, raw codfish, tomatoes, onions, sweet peppers, and celery.

Callaloo soup is made from okra, crabmeat, the spinach-like vegetable that gives the dish its name, and seasonings.

Christophines and **eddoes** are tasty, potatolike vegetables often served with curried shrimp, chicken, or goat.

Conkies are a mixture of cornmeal and coconut, pumpkin, raisins, sweet potatoes, and spices served wrapped in a banana leaf.

Cou-cou is a mix of cornmeal and okra with a spicy Creole sauce made from tomatoes, onions, and sweet peppers; it is often served with steamed flying fish.

Pepper-pot stew, a hearty mix of oxtail, beef chunks, and "any other meat you may have," simmered overnight, is flavored with *cassareep,* an ancient preservative and seasoning that gives the stew its dark, rich color.

Most menus include dolphinfish, kingfish, snapper, and flying fish prepared every way imaginable. Flying fish is a Bajan delicacy—so popular it has become a national symbol. Shellfish abounds; on the other hand, so does steak. For breakfast and dessert you'll find mangoes, soursop, papaya (pawpaw), and, in season, softball-size "mammy apples," a sweet, thick-skinned fruit with giant seeds.

Among the liquid refreshments of Barbados, there are, in addition to the local and omnipresent Banks beer and Mount Gay rum, **falernum** (a liqueur concocted of rum, sugar, lime juice, and almond essence) and **mauby** (a non-alcoholic drink made by boiling bitter bark and spices, straining the mixture, and sweetening it).

What to Wear

Barbados's British heritage and large resident population keep the dress code rather conservative and, on occasion, more formal than it is on neighboring islands. This can mean a jacket and tie for gentlemen and a cocktail dress for ladies in some restaurants. Other places are more casual, although you'll find jeans, shorts, and beach attire frowned upon at dinnertime.

CATEGORY	COST*
$$$	over $40
$$	$25–$40
$	under $25

per person for a three-course meal, excluding drinks and 10% service charge

$$$ ✕ **Bagatelle Great House.** The restored plantation house (circa 1645) that houses one of the oldest restaurants in Barbados is designated a "house of architectural and historical interest" by the Barbados National Trust. French and Caribbean cuisine is served for a light lunch or elegant dinner. Inside the castlelike walls, the ambience is romantic and very much like a private Colonial home. For more intimate dining, the garden terrace offers tables for two. Upstairs is a gallery of Caribbean art, a craft showroom, and a gift shop. ⊠ *Hwy. 2A, St. Thomas,* ☎ *246/421–6767. Reservations essential. AE, MC, V.*

$$$ ✕ **Carambola.** Dramatic lighting and a cliff-side setting
★ overlooking the Caribbean make this alfresco restaurant in St. James one of the most romantic on the island. It also serves some of the best food. The menu is a mix of Asian and classic French cuisine with a Caribbean touch. Start with a spicy, Caribbean-style crab tart, served with

hollandaise sauce on a bed of sweet pepper coulis. For an entrée, try fillet of kingfish broiled with ginger, coriander, and spring onions, or sliced duck breast with a wild mushroom fumet served with stuffed tomatoes and *gratin dauphinoise* (potatoes au gratin). When you think you can't eat another bite, the *citron gâteau* (lime mousse on a bed of lemon coulis) is a wonderfully light finish. ⊠ *Derricks, St. James,* ☎ *246/432–0832. Reservations essential. AE, MC, V. Closed Sun. No lunch.*

$$$ ✕ **Christophenes.** This elegant restaurant in the Royal Westmoreland Club House offers a lovely atmosphere and fine cuisine. The menu is diverse, if only because it is the inspiration of two chefs—one French, one Barbadian. Enjoy a truly gourmet experience at dinner, or enjoy a lighter repast at lunch. Early-bird golfers may grab a bite of breakfast before or after their 18 holes. ⊠ *St. James,* ☎ *246/422–4653. Reservations essential. AE, MC, V.*

$$$ ✕ **The Cliff.** Chef Paul Owens and manager Manuel
★   Ward have created one of the finest dining establishments in Barbados. Imaginative art accents the candlelit dining room, and every table has a view of the sea. The artistic mood extends to the innovative menu, which offers selections of excellent cuts of meat and fresh fish, creatively presented and accompanied by the freshest vegetables and greens you'll find anywhere. Don't skip dessert, which falls in the "sinful" category. ⊠ *Derricks, St. James,* ☎ *246/432–1922. AE, DC, MC, V. No lunch.*

$$$ ✕ **La Maison.** This restaurant, in a colonial-style man-
★   sion, Balmore House, exudes elegance with its English country furnishings and paneled bar opening onto a beachfront dining terrace. The mood is set for the terrific gourmet cuisine. A French chef, from the Loire Valley, creates seafood specials, including a flying-fish parfait appetizer. Passion-fruit ice cream is a dessert special. ⊠ *Holetown, St. James,* ☎ *246/432–1156. AE, DC, MC, V. Closed Mon.*

$$$ ✕ **Palm Terrace.** The Palm's French executive chef and his team apply their talents to an international à la carte menu that combines Barbadian produce with top-quality imports. The result is modern European creations, such as mille-feuille of home-smoked chicken with tomato, chives, and carrots in a light mustard cream sauce. Fresh mint accents New Zealand rack of lamb, and panfried crab becomes a stuffing for the breast of chicken entrée. Each evening there is a roast from the carvery. Widely spaced tables, comfortable chairs, and palms swaying under floor-to-ceiling arches creates a formal yet relaxed ambience as you dine facing the Caribbean Sea. ⊠ *Royal Pavilion Hotel, Porters, St. James,* ☎ *246/422–4444. AE, DC, MC, V. Closed Sun. No lunch.*

$$$ ✕ **Sandy Bay Restaurant.** The renowned Sandy Lane
★ Hotel is the perfect place for an elegant meal overlooking one of the best beaches on the island. Munich-born chef Hans Schweitzer, formerly of the Midsummer House in Cambridge, England, has modernized the cuisine by introducing *art culinair* to this historic resort. Dishes on the table d'hôte menu are mostly light fare, elegantly dressed with silky sauces, and accented with fresh vegetables. Grilled dolphinfish, lobster and shrimp tempura, and lamb with honey, thyme, and wild rosemary are among the entrées. Friday night, there's an international buffet. To secure the best produce, a van scours the island every morning for the freshest vegetables and fish. Desserts are French, creamy, and delicious. Be sure to dress for the occasion. ⊠ *Sandy Lane Hotel and Golf Club, St. James,* ☎ *246/432–1311. Reservations essential. AE, MC, V.*

$$ ✕ **Brown Sugar.** A special-occasion atmosphere prevails at Brown Sugar, set in a restored West Indian wooden house across from the Grand Barbados Beach Resort outside Bridgetown. Dozens of ferns and hanging plants decorate the breezy multilevel restaurant. An extensive and authentic West Indian lunch buffet (noon to 2:30)—from cou-cou to pepper-pot stew—is popular with local businesspeople. Dinner entrées include charbroiled ginger beef, Creole orange chicken, and homemade desserts, such as angel-food chocolate mousse cake, passion-fruit or nutmeg ice cream, and lime cheesecake. ⊠ *Aquatic*

24

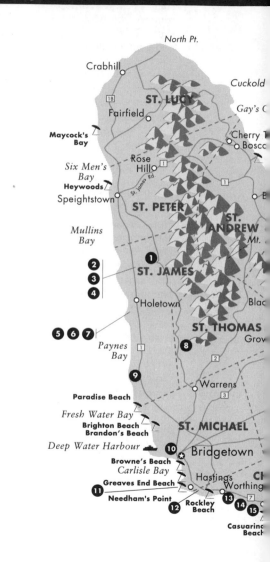

Dining

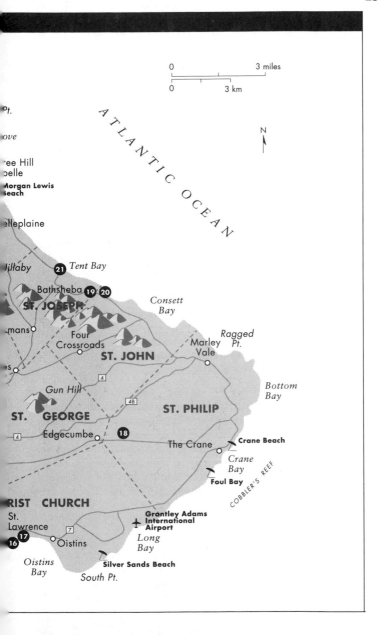

0   3 miles

0   3 km

ATLANTIC OCEAN

N

Pt.

ove

ee Hill
belle
**Morgan Lewis
Beach**

elleplaine

illaby   **21** *Tent Bay*

Bathsheba **19 20**

ST. JOSEPH   *Consett
Bay*

mans

Four
Crossroads

ST. JOHN   Marley
Vale   *Ragged
Pt.*

Gun Hill

*Bottom
Bay*

ST. GEORGE   **ST. PHILIP**

Edgecumbe   **18**

The Crane   **Crane Beach**

*Crane
Bay*

Foul Bay

COBBLER'S REEF

RIST CHURCH

St.
Lawrence

16 17   Oistins

**Grantley Adams
International
Airport**

*Long
Bay*

*Oistins
Bay*

Silver Sands Beach

South Pt.

Gap, Bay St., St. Michael, ☎ *246/426–7684. AE, DC, MC, V. No lunch Sat.*

$$ ✕ **Fathoms.** Veteran restaurateurs Stephen and Sandra Toppin open Fathoms beach restaurant seven days a week for lunch and dinner. Its 22 well-dressed tables are scattered from the inside dining rooms to the patio's ocean edge. Dinner may bring a grilled lobster, local rabbit, jumbo baked shrimp, or cashew-crusted kingfish. In the evenings, you can also grab a drink, a bite to eat, and a game of pool at Canyons, the upstairs bar. Fathoms is casual by day, candlelit by night. ⊠ *Paynes Bay, St. James,* ☎ *246/432–2568. AE, MC, V.*

$$ ✕ **Ile de France.** French owners Martine (from Lyon)
★ and Michel (the chef, from Toulouse) Gramaglia have turned the pool and garden areas of the Windsor Hotel into an island "in" spot. White latticework opens to the night sounds, soft French music plays, and a single, perfect hibiscus dresses each table. Among the classic French selections, the menu features delicately flavored Caribbean seafood and fabulous desserts—tarte Tatin, crème brûlée, and their original banana terrine. If you yearn for classic French cuisine, this is the place to be. ⊠ *Windsor Hotel, South Coast Main Rd., Hastings, Christ Church,* ☎ *246/435–6869. Reservations essential. MC, V. Closed Mon. No lunch.*

$$ ✕ **Josef's.** Swede Nils Ryman successfully created a menu from the unusual combination of Caribbean and Scandinavian fare. That, of course, means great fresh fish and seafood, including local lobster from the island's rocky east coast, and toast Skagen, made from diced shrimp blended with mayonnaise and fresh dill. Stroll around the garden before moving to the alfresco dining room downstairs or to the simply decorated room upstairs for a table that looks out over the sea. ⊠ *Waverly House, St. Lawrence Gap, Christ Church,* ☎ *246/435–6541. AE, MC, V.*

$$ ✕ **Pisces.** Fish is the way to go at this excellent water-
★ front restaurant in lively St. Lawrence Gap. Flying fish, dolphinfish, crab, kingfish, shrimp, prawns, and lobster are prepared any way from charbroiled to sautéed.

There are also some chicken and beef dishes. Other specialties include conch fritters, tropical *gazpacho* (cold, tomato-based soup) and seafood terrine with a mango sauce. The homemade rum raisin ice cream is a top choice for dessert. Enjoy your meal in a contemporary setting filled with hanging tropical plants and twinkling white lights that reflect on the water. ⊠ *St. Lawrence Gap, Christ Church,* ☎ *246/435–6564. AE, DC, MC, V. No lunch.*

$$ ✕ **Plantation Restaurant and Garden Theater.** The Bajan buffet and entertainment on Wednesday and Friday are big attractions here (☞ Chapter 7). The Plantation is in a renovated Barbadian residence surrounded by spacious grounds above the Southwinds Resort. Barbadian cuisine is served either indoors or on the terrace. ⊠ *St. Lawrence Rd., Christ Church,* ☎ *246/428–5048. AE, MC, V. No lunch.*

$$ ✕ **Rose and Crown.** A variety of fresh seafood is served in this casual eatery, but it's the local lobster that's high on diners' lists. Indoors is a paneled bar; outdoors are tables on a wraparound porch. ⊠ *Prospect, St. James,* ☎ *246/425–1074. AE, MC, V. Closed Sat. No lunch.*

$$ ✕ **Witch Doctor.** The interior of Witch Doctor is decorated with pseudo-African art, which gives a lighthearted, carefree atmosphere to this casual hangout across the street from the sea. The sensible menu includes traditional Barbadian dishes, such as steamed flying fish with rice and vegetables, as well as American fare and seafood. ⊠ *St. Lawrence Gap, Christ Church,* ☎ *246/435–6581. MC, V. No lunch.*

$ ✕ **Atlantis Hotel.** The seemingly endless luncheon buffet and magnificent ocean view make this restaurant a real find. Under the direction of owner-chef Enid Maxwell, the staff serves up an enormous Bajan buffet daily, with pumpkin fritters, spinach cake, pickled breadfruit, fried flying fish, roast chicken, pepper-pot stew, and West Indian–style okra and eggplant. Homemade coconut pie tops the dessert list. All that for $12.50 per person, except for Sundays, when a few dishes are added to the groaning board and the price becomes $17.50.

✉ *Atlantis Hotel, Bathsheba, St. Joseph,* ☎ *246/433–9445. AE.*

$ ✕ Bonito Beach Bar & Restaurant. When you tour the rugged east coast, plan to arrive in Bathsheba at lunchtime and stop at Mrs. Enid Worrell's Bonito Beach Bar for wholesome West Indian home cooking. The view of the Atlantic coast from the second-floor dining room of this otherwise plain restaurant is magnificent. Lunch might be a choice of fried fish, baked chicken, or beef stew, accompanied by local vegetables and salads fresh from the family garden. If your timing is right, Mrs. Worrell may have homemade cheesecake for dessert. Be sure to try the fresh fruit punch—with or without rum. The Bajan luncheon buffet, on Wednesdays and Sundays from 1 to 3, is popular. ✉ *Coast Rd., Bathsheba, St. Joseph,* ☎ *246/433–9034. No credit cards.*

$ ✕ David's Place. Come here for first-rate food in a first-rate location—a black-and-white Bajan cottage overlooking St. Lawrence Bay. Waves slap against the pilings of the open-air deck, providing a rhythmic accompaniment to your authentic Barbadian meal. The specialties—local flying fish, pepper-pot stew, curried shrimp—and other entrées, including a vegetarian platter, come with homemade cheese bread. Dessert might be banana pudding, carrot cake with rum sauce, or a cakelike dessert called cassava pone. ✉ *St. Lawrence Main Rd., Worthing, Christ Church,* ☎ *246/435–9755. AE, MC, V. Closed Mon.*

$ ✕ Edgewater Inn. You'll step into truly natural surroundings here, a perfect luncheon stop when touring the East Coast. The inn is surrounded by an 85-acre rain forest, a national park, and a river. It overlooks 9 mi of beach, including Barbados's famed Soup Bowl. The dining room is furnished with tables and chairs hand-carved from local mahogany. Meanwhile, you can enjoy light fare of sandwiches, salads, and French-bread pizzas or a traditional Bajan feast and dessert buffet. Dinners are also served, but mostly it's inn guests who partake. ✉ *Bathsheba, St. Joseph,* ☎ *246/433–9900. AE, MC, V.*

$ ✕ **Sunbury Plantation House.** In the Courtyard Restau-
★ rant, on a patio surrounded by beautiful gardens, lun-
cheon is served to visitors as part of the house tour (if
you wish). The Bajan buffet includes chicken and fish,
salads, rice and peas, and steamed local vegetables. Tri-
fle, pastries, and ice cream are dessert choices. Sandwiches
and other à la carte items are available, too. A special
mood is created in the evening, when small groups dine
in the plantation-house dining room. ⊠ *St. Philip,* ☎
246/423–6270. Reservations essential. AE, MC, V.

$ ✕ **Waterfront Cafe.** Facing the busy harbor in
Bridgetown, this friendly bistro is the perfect place to
enjoy a drink, snack, or meal. Locals and tourists gather
at outdoor café tables for sandwiches, salads, fish, pasta,
pepper-pot stew, and tasty Bajan snacks. The panfried
flying-fish sandwich is especially popular. In the evening,
from the brick and mirrored interior, you can gaze
through the arched windows while you savor '90s-style
Creole cuisine, enjoy the cool trade winds, listen to the
live music, and let time pass. ⊠ *The Careenage,
Bridgetown, St. Michael,* ☎ *246/427–0093. AE, DC,
MC, V. Closed Sun.*

4 Beaches

BARBADOS BEACHES are all open to the public. Although nonguests may not always have immediate access to hotel beaches, you can walk onto almost any beach from an adjacent one. Beaches on the West Coast have gentle Caribbean surf and are shaded by leafy mahogany trees. South Coast beaches, dotted with tall palms, have medium-to-high surf; the waves get bigger the farther southeast you go. On east-coast beaches, the Atlantic Ocean surf can be rough with a strong undertow, so swimming and surfing are risky there.

Sunbathing

Just plain basking is one of the great pleasures of a Caribbean vacation, but before abandoning yourself to the tropics, you would be well advised to take precautions against the ravages of its equatorial sun. Be sure to use a sunscreen with a sun-protection factor, or SPF, of at least 15; if you're engaging in water sports, be sure the sunscreen is waterproof. At this latitude, the safest hours for sunbathing are 4–6 PM, but even then it is wise to limit exposure during your first few days to 15–20 minutes. Keep your system plied with fruit juices and water, and avoid coffee, tea, and alcohol, which hasten the dehydration process.

West Coast Beaches

The West Coast has the stunning coves and white-sand beaches that are dear to postcard publishers—plus calm, clear water for snorkeling, scuba diving, and swimming. The salt water will buoy you—making floating almost effortless. West Coast beaches continue almost unbroken from Almond Beach Village in the north down to Bridgetown. Elegant private homes and luxury hotels take up most of the beachfront property in this area, which is why this stretch of sandy shoreline is called Barbados's Gold Coast.

Although West Coast beaches are seldom crowded, they are not the place to find isolation. Owners of private boats stroll by, offering waterskiing, parasailing, and snorkel cruises. There are no concession stands, but hotels welcome nonguests for terrace lunches (wear a cover-up). Picnic items and necessities can be bought at the Sunset Crest shopping center in Holetown. The afternoon clouds and sunsets are breathtaking from any of the West Coast beaches.

Brighton Beach, just north of Bridgetown, is not far from the port. It's a large beach, with a beach bar; and being close to town, it's a favorite for locals.

Mullins Beach, south of Speightstown at Mullins Bay, is a good place for a swim and is safe for snorkeling. There's easy parking on the main road, and when you want a break from the sun, Mullins Beach Bar has snacks and drinks.

Paynes Bay, south of Holetown, is the site of a number of luxury hotels. It's a very pretty area, with plenty of beach to go around. Parking areas and access are available opposite the Coach House Pub. Grab a bite to eat at Bomba's Beach Bar.

South Coast Beaches

South Coast beaches are much busier than those on the West Coast and generally draw a younger, more active crowd. The quality of the beach itself is consistently good; the reef-protected waters are safe for swimming and snorkeling.

Accra Beach, in Rockley, is very popular. There are lots of people, lots of activity, food and drink nearby, and rental equipment for snorkeling and other water sports. There's a car park at the beach.

The cove at **Bottom Bay,** north of Sam Lord's Castle, is lovely. Follow the steps down the cliff to a strip of white sand lined by coconut palms and faced by an aquamarine sea. There's even a cave to explore. It's out of the way and not near restaurants, so bring a picnic lunch.

Casuarina Beach, at the Casuarina Beach Club in the St. Lawrence Gap area, is a beach with lots of breeze and a fair amount of surf. Public access is from Maxwell Coast Road.

Where the South Coast meets the Atlantic side of the island, the waves roll in bigger and faster. **Crane Beach** has for years been a popular swimming beach, and the waves are a favorite with bodysurfers. This can be rough water, so exercise caution.

Foul Bay is ruggedly attractive and lives up to its name only for sailboats; for swimmers and alfresco lunches (pack your own picnic), it's perfect.

Greaves End Beach, south of Bridgetown at Aquatic Gap, between the Grand Barbados Beach Resort and the Barbados Hilton in St. Michael, is a good spot for swimming.

Needham's Point, with its lighthouse, is one of Barbados's best beaches. It's crowded with local people on weekends and holidays.

In Worthing, next to the Sandy Beach Island Resort, **Sandy Beach** has shallow, calm waters and a picturesque lagoon. It's an ideal location for families, with beach activities on weekends. There's parking on the main road and plenty of places nearby to buy food or drink.

Silver Sands Beach, close to the southern-most point of the island, has a beautiful expanse of white sand beach, with a stiff breeze that appeals to windsurfers.

East Coast Beaches

With long stretches of open beach and crashing ocean waves, rocky cliffs, and verdant hills, the windward side of Barbados won't disappoint anyone who seeks dramatic views. But be cautioned: Swimming at East Coast beaches is treacherous and *not* recommended. The waves are high, the bottom tends to be rocky, and the currents are unpredictable. Limit yourself to enjoying the view and watching the surfers—who have been at it since they were kids.

Miles of beach follow the wild coast at **Bathsheba and Cattlewash,** where the pounding surf of the Atlantic is mesmerizing. This is where Barbadians keep second homes and spend holidays. Swimming in these waters can be extremely dangerous even for strong swimmers. Bring a picnic or have lunch at one of the local restaurants with a view.

A worthwhile, little-visited beach for those who don't mind trekking about a mile off the beaten path, **Morgan Lewis**

Beach is east of Morgan Lewis Mill, the oldest intact wind-mill on the island. Turn east on the small road that goes to the town of Boscobelle (between Cherry Tree Hill and Morgan Lewis Mill); but instead of going to town, take the even less-traveled road (unmarked on most maps; you will have to ask for directions) that goes down the cliff to the beach. What awaits is more than 2 mi of unspoiled, unin-habited white sand and sweeping views of the Atlantic coastline. You may see a few Barbadians swimming, sun-ning, or fishing, but for the most part you'll have privacy.

5 Outdoor Activities and Sports

OUTDOOR ACTIVITIES

Fishing

Blue Jay Charters (☎ 246/422–2098) has a 45-ft, fully equipped fishing boat, with a crew that knows the waters where blue marlin, sailfish, barracuda, and kingfish play.

Golfing

Barbadians love golf, and golfers love Barbados. Greens fees range from $12.50 for nine holes at Belair to $145 for 18 holes at Royal Westmoreland Golf Club.

Almond Beach Village (☎ 246/422–4900), on the northwest corner of the island, has a nine-hole executive course for guest use only; clubs are provided. The **Belair Par-3** (☎ 246/423–4653) course is on the rugged East Coast, near Sam Lord's Castle. **Club Rockley Barbados** (☎ 246/435–7873), on the South Coast, has a challenging nine-hole course. The **Royal Westmoreland Golf Club** (☎ 246/422–4653) has a world-class Robert Trent Jones Jr. 18-hole course that meanders through the 500-acre Westmoreland Sugar Estate, past million-dollar villas, and overlooks the scenic West Coast. Nine additional holes are under way. To play here, you must stay at a hotel with access privileges. The prestigious **Sandy Lane Club** (☎ 246/432–1145) has a challenging 18-hole championship course. The dramatic 11th hole is famous for both its elevated tee and its incredible view.

Hiking

Hilly but not mountainous, the interior of Barbados is ideal for hiking. The **Barbados National Trust** (⊠ No. 2, 10th Ave., Belleville, St. Michael, ☎ 246/436–9033) sponsors free 5-mi walks year-round on Sunday, from 6 AM to about 9:30 AM and from 3:30 PM to 5:30 PM, as well as special moonlight hikes when the heavens permit. Newspapers announce the time and meeting place (or you can call the Trust).

Horseback Riding

The **Caribbean International Riding Center** (✉ Auburn, St. Joseph, ☎ 246/433–1453 or 246/420–1246) offers one-hour rides through nearby gullies for $27.50 and a special ride through the countryside to Villa Nova Great House, including lunch and a tour of the house, for $187.50; transportation to and from your hotel is included. On the West Coast, **Brighton Stables** (✉ Black Rock, St. Michael, ☎ 246/425–9381) offers one-hour rides along beaches and palm groves for $27.50, including transportation.

Parasailing

Parasailing is available, wind conditions permitting, on the beaches of St. James and Christ Church. It involves strapping on a parachute-like contraption and letting a speedboat tow you until you're gliding through the air. **Skyrider Parasail** (☎ 246/420–6362) operates from Bay Street in Bridgetown, but the boat does pickups all along the West Coast. Just flag down the speedboat, though the operator may find you first. Rates are $45 per flight—and they even take credit cards (MasterCard and Visa). Children and the physically challenged present no problem.

Sailing Excursions

Party boats depart from the Careenage or Bridgetown Harbour area. For around $55, lunchtime snorkeling and cocktail-hour sunset catamaran cruises are available on **Limbo Lady** (☎ 246/420–5418) and on **Irish Mist, Spirit of Barbados, Tiami II,** and **Tropical Dreamer** (☎ 246/427–7245). **Secret Love** (☎ 246/432–1972), a 41-ft Morgan sailboat, offers daily lunchtime or evening snorkel cruises.

The red-sailed **Jolly Roger** "pirate" party ship makes lunch-and-rum cruises along the West Coast for $52 (✉ Fun Cruises, ☎ 246/436–6424).

A motor vessel rather than a sailboat, the 100-ft M/V **Harbour Master** has four decks, fun and games, food and drink, and an adventurous spirit. It can land on beaches to access many hotels; you can view the briny deep from its onboard 34-seat semisubmersible. It leaves Bridgetown for four- and five-hour cruises along the West Coast, stopping in Holetown and at beaches along the way. ☎ *246/430–0900.* *$50.* *Tues. and Thurs.–Sat.*

Scuba Diving

Dive sites are concentrated along the West Coast, between Bridgetown and Maycocks Bay, St. Lucy. Certified divers can explore reefs, wrecks, and the walls of "blue holes," the huge circular depressions in the ocean floor. Underwater visibility is generally 80–90 ft. Not to be missed is the *Stavronikita,* a 356-ft Greek freighter that was deliberately sunk at about 135 ft off St. James beach; hundreds of butterfly fish hang out around its mast, and the thin rays of sunlight that filter down through the water make exploring the huge ship a wonderfully eerie experience. Virtually every part of the ship is accessible. A one-tank dive runs about $40–$45; two-tank, $50–$55.

While scuba (which stands for self-contained underwater breathing apparatus) looks and is surprisingly simple, *call your physician before your vacation and make sure that you have no condition that should prevent you from diving!* A full checkup is an excellent idea, especially if you're over 30. Since it can be dangerous to travel on a plane after diving, you should schedule both your diving courses and travel plans accordingly.

Learning to dive with a reputable instructor is also a must. In addition to training you how to resurface slowly enough, a qualified instructor can teach you to read "dive tables," the charts that calculate how long you can safely stay at certain depths.

Many dive shops provide instruction in scuba diving—a three-hour beginner's "resort" course (about $75) or a weeklong certification course (about $350), followed by a shallow dive—usually on Dottin's Reef, off Holetown.

Successful completion of this introductory course may prompt you to do further course work to earn a certification card—often called a C-card—from one of the major accredited diving organizations: NAUI (National Associa-

In case you want to see the world.

In case you want to be welcomed there.

We're here to see that you're always welcomed at establishments everywhere. That's why millions of people carry the American Express® Card – for peace of mind, confidence, and security, around the world or just around the corner.

do more ®

AMERICAN EXPRESS

Cards

In case you're running low.

We're here to help with more than 118,000 Express Cash locations around the world. In order to enroll, just call American Express before you start your vacation.

do more

And just in case.

We're here with American Express® Travelers Cheques and Cheques *for Two*.® They're the safest way to carry money on your vacation and the surest way to get a refund, practically anywhere, anytime.
Another way we help you...

do more®

AMERICAN
EXPRESS

Travelers
Cheques

tion of Underwater Instructors), CMAS (Confederation Mondiale des Activités Subaquatiques, which translates into World Underwater Federation), NASE (National Association of Scuba Educators), or PADI (Professional Association of Diving Instructors). PADI offers a free list of training facilities (⊠ 1251 E. Dyer Rd., #100, Santa Ana, CA 92705).

Barbados has a **decompression chamber,** based at the Barbados Defence Force Dive Accident Unit (⊠ St. Ann's Fort, St. Michael, ☎ 246/436–6185), available to divers on a 24-hour basis.

Dive Boat Safari (⊠ Barbados Hilton, St. Michael, ☎ 246/427–4350) offers full diving and instruction services. The **Dive Shop, Ltd.** (⊠ Aquatic Gap, near Grand Barbados Beach Resort, St. Michael, ☎ 246/426–9947) has one- and two-tank dive trips, or you can purchase a six-dive package. **Exploresub Barbados** (⊠ St. Lawrence Gap, Christ Church, ☎ 246/435–6542) is a PADI five-star training facility that offers a full range of daily dives. **Hightide** (⊠ Sandy Lane Hotel, St. James, ☎ 246/432–0931) offers one- and two-tank dives, night reef/wreck/drift dives, the full range of PADI instruction, and free transportation.

Snorkeling

Snorkeling requires no special skills, and most hotels that rent equipment have a staff member or, at the very least, a booklet offering instruction in snorkeling basics.

As with any water sport, it's never good to go alone, especially if you're out of shape. You don't have to be a great swimmer to snorkel, but occasionally currents come up that require stamina. The four dimensions as we know them seem altered underwater. Time seems to slow and stand still, so wear a water-resistant watch and let someone on land know when to expect you back.

Remember that taking souvenirs—shells, pieces of coral, interesting rocks—is forbidden. Many reefs are legally protected marine parks, where removal of living shells is prohibited because it upsets the ecology.

Gear for snorkeling can be rented for a small charge from nearly every hotel. Snorkelers can usually accompany dive trips for about $20 for a two-hour trip (☞ Scuba Diving, *above*).

Squash

Accra Beach Hotel and Resort (⊠ Rockley, Christ Church, ☎ 246/435–8920) and **Almond Beach Village** (⊠ St. Peter, ☎ 246/422–4900) offer squash to guests. At **Club Rockley Barbados** (⊠ Rockley, Christ Church, ☎ 246/435–7880) nonguests can reserve courts for $10 per hour. At the **Barbados Squash Club** (⊠ Marine House, Christ Church, ☎ 246/427–7913), courts can be reserved at the rate of $9 for 45 minutes.

Submarining

Minisubmarine voyages are enormously popular with families and those who enjoy watching fish without getting wet. The great-for-kids, 48-passenger **Atlantis III** turns the Caribbean into a giant aquarium. The 45-minute trip aboard the Canadian-built, 50-ft submarine takes you to wrecks and reefs as deep as 150 ft below the surface for a look at what even sport divers rarely see. The nighttime dives, using high-power searchlights, are spectacular. Classical music plays while an oceanography specialist informs during both day and night dives, either of which last about 90 minutes. ⊠ *Bridgetown Harbour, Spring Garden Hwy.,* ☎ *246/436–8929.* ⌑ *$70.*

Children will love the **Atlantis SEATREC** (Sea Tracking and Reef Exploration Craft), which allows passengers to "snorkel without getting wet!" The 46-passenger vessel has large viewing windows 6 ft below the surface where you can stay dry and still view the underwater marine life on a near-shore reef. ⊠ *Bridgetown Harbour, Spring Garden Hwy.,* ☎ *246/436–8929.* ⌑ *$29.50.*

Surfing

The best surfing is available on the East Coast, and most wave riders congregate at the Soup Bowl, near Bathsheba.

An annual international surfing competition is held on Barbados every September, when the surf is at its peak.

Tennis

Most hotels have tennis courts that can be reserved day and night. Be sure to pack your whites, as appropriate dress is expected on the court. Public courts are available with no fee and no reservations at **Folkestone Park** (✉ Holetown, ☎ 246/422–2314) and at the **National Tennis Centre** (✉ Sir Garfield Sobers Sports Complex, Wildey, St. Michael, ☎ 246/437–6010) for $12 per hour with reservations.

Waterskiing

Waterskiing is offered through **Blue Reef Watersports** at the Royal Pavilion Hotel, St. James (☎ 246/422–4444). Private speedboat owners have several ski sizes and troll for business on the waterfront in St. James and Christ Church; they will offer their services through a hotel or directly to vacationers or can be hailed like taxis. Ask your hotel staff or other guests about their experiences with these entrepreneurs: Keep in mind that with these independent operators, you water-ski at your own risk. Be *sure* they provide life vests and at least two people in the boat: one to drive and one to watch the skier at all times.

Windsurfing

Windsurfing is as strenuous as it is exciting, so it may not be the sport to try on your first day out—unless, of course, you're already in excellent shape. Always windsurf with someone else around who can go for help if necessary.

The best places to windsurf are at **Club Mistral,** Silver Sands Hotel, Maxwell (☎ 246/428–7277), **Silver Rock Windsurfing Club,** Silver Rock Hotel, Silver Sands Beach (☎ 246/428–2866), and **Windsurf Village Barbados,** Maxwell (☎ 246/428–9095), all on the southeast coast of the island, where the Barbados Windsurfing Championships are held mid-January. Barbados ranks as one of the best locations in the world for windsurfing—part of the World Cup Windsurfing Circuit.

Windsurfing boards and equipment are often guest amenities at the larger hotels and can be rented by nonguests. The **Windsurf Village Barbados** (✉ Maxwell Main Rd., Christ Church, ☎ 246/428–9095) caters specifically to windsurfing aficionados.

SPECTATOR SPORTS

Cricket

The island is mad for cricket, and you can sample a match at almost any time of year. Although the season is from May through late December, test matches are usually played from January through April. The newspapers give the details of time and place and you can call **BCA/WICB** (☎ 246/429–6505 or 246/436–1397) for upcoming series information. Tickets to cricket matches at **Kensington Oval** range from $5 to $25.

Cricket is an extremely complex sport, but even a basic understanding of the rules renders the game enjoyable. It is played by two 11-member teams on a roughly circular pitch (playing surface) surrounded by a rope boundary. Most of the action, however, takes place on a central rectangle, 66 feet long. The batting team places two batsmen at opposite sides of the rectangle; a **wicket** (two wooden **bails** balanced horizontally atop three **stumps** of wood) stands behind each batsman. The objective of the batsman is twofold: to guard the wickets and to score runs. The fielding team's **bowler** (pitcher) at one end of the rectangle throws a ball to the batsman at the opposite end, attempting to "bowl" the batsman by knocking the bails off the stumps.

The ball is thrown overhand with a straight arm (bent elbows are penalized) and is usually bounced off the pitch, which has been hardened by rollers. The batsman attempts to hit the ball far enough that he and his batting partner can exchange places and score runs. There are no foul lines, so the ball may go in any direction. If the ball crosses the boundary on the ground, the batsman scores four runs; if it crosses the boundary without touching the ground, six runs are scored. The batsman's "wicket is taken" (he's

out) if the bails are knocked off the stumps while the batsmen are "out of the crease" (changing places) or if his ball
is caught on the fly. Once a player's wicket is taken, he is
replaced.

An **over** (six throws) is bowled from one end of the rectangle; then another bowler takes over from the other end
and the fielders rotate accordingly. The batting team remains
at bat until 10 wickets have been taken (the end of an "in-
nings") or until they "declare" (decide to stop batting and
take the field). A team will declare because, to win, they
must not only score the most runs but also take all of the
opposing side's wickets by the scheduled end of the game.
The length of a match varies widely: Limited over matches
have a set number of overs and are usually one-day events;
other matches last four days. International test matches last
up to five days.

If you're confused, ask another spectator—he or she will
probably enjoy sharing some knowledge.

Horse Racing

Horse racing takes place on alternate Saturdays, from January to March and May to December, at the **Garrison Savannah** in Christ Church, about 3 mi south of Bridgetown.
The Sandy Lane Gold Cup in March draws top class horses
from Barbados, Martinique, Trinidad and Tobago. ⊠ *Christ
Church,* ☎ *246/426–3980.* ☞ *$5.* ☉ *1:30 on race days.*

Polo

Polo matches are held at the **Polo Club** in Holders Hill, St.
James (☎ 246/432–1802 or 246/421–6852), on Wednes-
days and Saturdays from September to March for about
$2.50. Dress smartly and hang around the club room after
the match. That's where the lies, the legends, and the in-
vitations happen.

Rugby

The rough-and-tumble game of rugby is played at the Garrison Savannah (☞ Horse Racing, *above*), and touring

teams are always welcome; schedules are available from the **Barbados Rugby Club.** Contact Victor Roach (☎ 246/435–6543).

Soccer

The soccer (or football, as it's called here) season runs from January through June at National Stadium. For game information contact the **Barbados Football Association** (✉ Box 1362, Belleville, St. Michael, ☎ 246/228–1707 or 246/228–0149).

6 Shopping

TRADITIONALLY, **BROAD STREET** and its side
streets in Bridgetown have been the center for shopping. Stores are known for
their high-quality merchandise, good service, and excellent
value. Hours are generally weekdays 9–5 and Saturday 8–
1. Branches of the largest Broad Street fashion and department stores are at the Cruise Ship Terminal, at the
airport, and in large hotels. There are two **Chattel House
Village** complexes (⊠ St. Lawrence Gap; Holetown), each
a cluster of brightly colored shops where you can buy local
products, rums and liqueurs, hand-designed clothing, beachwear, and souvenirs. At the **Cruise Ship Terminal** shopping
mall, cruise-ship passengers can buy both duty-free goods
and Barbadian-made merchandise at dozens of shops, bou-
tiques, and vendor carts and stalls. **DaCostas Mall** (⊠ Broad
St., Bridgetown) has 35 shops that sell everything from Pi-
aget to postcards. The **Quayside Shopping Center** (⊠ Rockley, Christ Church, ☎ 246/428–2474) is small but has a
group of exclusive shops.

Antiques

Barbadian and British antiques and fine memorabilia are
the stock of **Greenwich House Antiques** (⊠ Greenwich Village, Trents Hill, St. James, ☎ 246/432–1169). It's a whole
plantation house full of antique Barbadian mahogany furniture, crystal, silver, china, and pictures and is open daily
from 10:30 AM to 6 PM.

Antiquaria (⊠ Spring Garden Hwy., St. Michael's Row,
Bridgetown, ☎ 246/426–0635), a pink Victorian house next
to the Anglican cathedral, sells antique silver, brass items,
mahogany furniture, and maps and engravings of Barbados. A branch is in Holetown, St. James (☎ 246/432–2647),
opposite Sandpiper Inn. They're both open every day but
Sunday.

Boutiques

Coconut Junction & Lazy Days (⊠ Quayside Shopping Center, Rockley, ☎ 246/435–8115), actually two shops in

one, have top-quality beachwear, beach accessories, and beach equipment—including surf and boogie boards.

Carol Cadogan's **Cotton Days Designs** (⊠ Ramsgate Cottage, Lower Bay St., ☎ 246/427–7191) is a very upscale shop that sets the international pace with all-cotton collage creations that have been declared "wearable art." These are fantasy designs, with prices that begin around $250. Fortunately, she takes credit cards.

Another shop worth a visit is **Origins—Colours of the Caribbean** (⊠ The Careenage, ☎ 246/436–8522), where original hand-painted and batik clothing, imported cottons, linens and silks for day and evening, and handmade jewelry and accessories are the order of the day. The hand-painted T-shirt dresses, priced at about $100, are fabulous.

Signatures (⊠ Broad St., Bridgetown, ☎ 246/431–5577) specializes in cosmetics, fragrances, and skin care. On the first floor, the Beauty Spa offers facials, massages, and consultations.

At **Sunny Shoes Inc.** (⊠ Cave Shepherd, Broad St., ☎ 246/431–2121) concessionaire DeCourcey Clarke will make a pair of women's strap sandals while you wait—in any color(s) you wish—for $26–$30.

Duty-Free Luxury Goods

Bridgetown's Broad Street stores offer duty-free values on luxury goods, such as fine bone china, crystal, cameras, porcelain, leather, stereo and video equipment, jewelry, perfume, and clothing. Prices for many items are often 30%–50% less than those back home. In order to purchase items duty-free, visitors must produce ongoing travel tickets and a passport at the time of purchase—or you can have your purchases delivered free to the airport or harbor for pickup. Duty-free alcohol and tobacco products *must* be delivered to you at the airport or harbor.

Cave Shepherd (☎ 246/431–2121), the island's only true department store, offers a wide selection of tax-free luxury goods at five locations, including Broad Street, the airport, and the Cruise Ship Terminal.

Correia's (⌧ Prince William Henry St., ☎ 246/429–5985), just off Broad Street, sells gold, diamond, and gemstone jewelry and watches—at 30% less than U.S. retail—under the watchful eye of Maurice and Marcelle Correia, certified gemologists.

De Lima's (⌧ 20 Broad St., ☎ 246/426–4644) is the centerpiece of its own small mall and stocks high-quality imports. Among the specialty shops here are several jewelry stores and a few crafts stores.

Harrison's is a large specialty retailer with 11 locations on the island, including two large stores on Broad Street. Luxury name-brand goods from the fashion corners of the world are available at duty-free prices.

Louis Bayley is one of the fine shops at DaCosta's Mall, on Broad Street (☎ 246/430–4842), and has six other locations. You'll find perfume, jewelry and fine watches, cameras and audio equipment, Swarovski and Waterford crystal, and Wedgwood china at duty-free prices.

The Royal Shop (⌧ 32–34 Broad St., ☎ 246/429–7072) carries fine watches and jewelry fashioned in Italian gold, Caribbean silver, diamonds, and other gemstones.

Handicrafts

Island handicrafts are everywhere: woven mats and place mats, dresses, dolls, handbags, shell jewelry, wooden carvings, and local artwork.

Best 'n the Bunch (⌧ St. Lawrence Gap, ☎ 246/428–2474) is in a brightly painted building at the Chattel House Village. Look here for jewelry designed and crafted by Bajan David Trottman.

The **Best of Barbados** shops (⌧ Mall 34, Broad St., Bridgetown, ☎ 246/436–1416, and 11 other locations) offer the highest-quality artwork and crafts, both "native style" and modern designs. A local artist, Jill Walker, sells her watercolors and prints here.

Earthworks (⌧ Edgehill Heights, No. 2, St. Thomas, ☎ 246/425–0223) is a family-owned and -operated pottery where you can purchase anything from a complete dinner service to a one-of-a-kind clay art piece.

Pelican Village (✉ Harbour Rd., between Cheapside Market and Bridgetown Harbour, ☎ 246/426–4391) offers bargains from local craftspeople. In a cluster of open-air, conical shops, you can watch as goods are crafted. Locally made handbags and leather goods, coconut-shell accessories, mahogany items, and grass rugs and mats are good buys.

For arts from Barbados and elsewhere in the Caribbean, visit the **Verandah Art Gallery** (✉ Broad St., Bridgetown, ☎ 246/426–2605).

At **Women's Self Help** (✉ Broad St., next to Nelson's Statue, ☎ 246/426–2570), you can find homemade embroidery and crochet work, shell art, baskets, children's clothes, jams and jellies, and candy.

7 Nightlife and the Arts

NIGHTLIFE

When the sun goes down, the musicians come out and folks go limin' (anything from hanging out to a chat-up or jump-up) in Barbados. Competitions among reggae groups, steel bands, and calypso singers are major events, and tickets can be hard to come by—but give it a try.

Bars and Inns

Barbados supports the rum industry in more than 1,600 "rum shops," simple bars where people (mostly men) congregate to discuss the world's ills, and in more sophisticated inns, where you'll find world-class rum drinks made with the island's renowned Mount Gay and Cockspur rums. In Barbados, rum means dark rum, so if you want the white stuff, you'll have to ask for it. Banks is the local beer.

Bert's Bar at the Abbeville Hotel (⊠ Rockley, Christ Church, ☎ 246/435–7924) serves the best daiquiris in town . . . any town. **The Boatyard** (⊠ Bay St., Bridgetown, ☎ 246/436–2622) stays open until the wee hours and is popular with both locals and visitors. **Bubba's Sports Bar** (⊠ Rockley Main Rd., Christ Church, ☎ 246/435–6217) has two satellite dishes, a 10-ft video screen, and 12 additional TVs where you can watch live sports action while sipping a Banks or enjoying a Bubba burger, or both. **Coach House** (⊠ Paynes Bay, St. James, ☎ 246/432–1163) is the only West Coast nightspot with live entertainment Tuesday through Saturday nights. Also try the friendly pub with live bands, **Ship Inn** (⊠ St. Lawrence Gap, Christ Church, ☎ 246/435–6961).

For the adventurous party-lover, a late-night (after 11) excursion to **Baxter Road,** "the street that never sleeps," is de rigueur for midnight Bajan street snacks, local rum, great gossip, and good storytelling. **Enid & Livy's** and **Collins** are just two of the long-standing favorite haunts.

Dancing

Wherever there is live music, dancing usually accompanies it, but here are two regular bets.

Harbour Lights, in a typical old Barbadian home, has a beachfront location. It claims to be the "home of the party animal" and, most any night, features dancing under the stars to live reggae and soca music. ⊠ *Marine Villa, Bay St., Bridgetown, St. Michael,* ☎ *246/436–7225.*

For a more refined evening, enjoy dancing to a steel band or a string quartet at Sandy Lane Hotel's **Starlight Terrace.** ⊠ *Hwy. 1, St. Peter,* ☎ *246/432–1311.*

Dinner Shows

Most of the large resorts have weekend shows for visitors, and there is a selection of dinner shows, which you can attend for the entire evening or for just the performance.

Club Xanadu is a mid-December–April cabaret. David McCarty, who danced on Broadway and with the New York City Ballet, has joined forces with chanteuse Jean Emerson; on Thursday and Friday nights along with local strutters, they put on the hottest show in town. Dinner—served in the upstairs flower-decked dining room—and show cost $44; cabaret admission only, approximately $12.50. ⊠ *Ocean View Hotel, Hastings,* ☎ *246/427–7821. Reservations essential.*

On Wednesday and Friday evenings at **Plantation Restaurant and Garden Theater,** the "Barbados Tropical Spectacular" calypso cabaret show features dancing, fire-eating, limbo, steel-band music, and the award-winning sounds of Spice & Company. The cost for a Barbadian cuisine dinner, unlimited drinks, transportation, and the show is $52.50; for the show and drinks only, you pay $25. ⊠ *St. Lawrence Rd., Christ Church,* ☎ *246/428–5048. AE, MC, V.*

The dinner show at the **Sherbourne Centre,** Barbados's convention center, is called "1627 and All That." It has a 17th-century Barbados theme and is performed by the energetic dancers of the Barbados Dance Theater. ⊠ *Two Mile*

Hill, east of Bridgetown, St. Michael, ☎ *246/431–7600.*
✉ *$50 for dinner, show, and open bar; $25 show only.*

Jazz

While there's plenty of hot entertainment venues geared for
visitors, you may also want to hit the locals' favorite
nightspots. The most popular one is still **After Dark** (✉ St.
Lawrence Gap, Christ Church, ☎ 246/435–6547), with the
longest bar on the island, a jazz-club annex, and an outdoor area where headliners perform. Stop in for an evening
of mellow jazz at **Cobbler's Cove.** (✉ Hwy. 1, St. Peter, ☎
246/422–2291), or the **Waterfront Cafe** (✉ The Careenage,
Bridgetown, ☎ 246/427–0093) for jazz and dancing.

THE ARTS

Galleries

Barbados Art Council. The gallery shows drawings, paintings, and other art, with a new show about every two
weeks. ✉ *2 Pelican Village, Harbour Rd., Bridgetown,* ☎
246/426–4385. ✉ *Free.* ☉ *Weekdays 10–5, Sat. 9–1.*

Barbados Gallery of Art (✉ The Garrison, Bush Hill, St.
Michael, ☎ 246/228–0149) opened in this location in
1996 with a permanent collection of 20th-century Barbadian and Caribbean fine art. Changing exhibitions are also
on view.

The **Natural Cultural Foundation Gallery** (✉ Queen's Park,
Bridgetown, ☎ 246/427–2345), the island's largest gallery,
is managed by the National Culture Foundation and presents monthlong exhibits.

A selection of private art galleries offers Bajan and West
Indian art at collectible prices. The **Studio Art Gallery** (✉
Fairchild St., Bridgetown, ☎ 246/427–5463) exhibits local
work (particularly that of Rachael Altman) and will frame
purchases.

Theater

Holder's Season. This organization's acclaimed season of opera and Shakespeare runs three weeks each year beginning in March. The open-air theater seats 600 and has presented headliners such as Luciano Pavarotti. A new opera for a steel drum band is planned for 1998. ⊠ *Holder's House, Holder's Hill, St. James,* ☎ *246/432–6385.*

8 Exploring Barbados

AS YOU WANDER from one of the island's 11 parishes to the next, the terrain and vegetation change dramatically—and so do the pace and ambience. The capital Bridgetown, in St. Michael, is a busy and sophisticated city. Gold Coast resorts and private homes in St. James and St. Peter ooze luxury, and the small villages and plantations scattered throughout the rest of central Barbados mark the island's history. The remote East Coast, with its cliffs and heavy surf, has been designed by the Atlantic Ocean. The ocean-whipped wildness and rich fields of the northeast, including the parishes of St. Andrew and St. Joseph, is referred to as Scotland for it's likeness. And, along the lively Christ Church South Coast, the energy continues day and night.

The Barbados National Trust, headquartered at 10th Avenue, Belleville, St. Michael (☎ 246/426–2421), has designed the **Heritage Passport,** a 50% discounted admission to Barbados's most popular attractions and historic sites. A Full Passport includes 16 sites and costs $35; a Mini-Passport includes five sites and costs $18. Children under 12 are admitted free if accompanied by a Passport holder (maximum two children per passport). Passports may be purchased at hotels, Trust headquarters, or at the sites.

Bridgetown

Bridgetown is a bustling city and a major Caribbean duty-free port. The principal thoroughfare is Broad Street, which leads west from Trafalgar Square. The busy capital is a maze of one-way streets complete with rush hours and traffic congestion. Sightseeing will take only an hour or so, and the shopping area is compact.

Numbers in the margin correspond to points of interest on the Exploring Bridgetown map.

Sights to See

🐚 ❽ **Barbados Museum.** This intriguing museum, in the former Military Prison, has artifacts from Arawak days (around 400 BC) and mementos of military history and everyday life in the 19th century. You'll see cane-harvesting implements, lace wedding dresses, ancient (and frightening) dentistry instruments, and slave sale accounts kept in a spidery copperplate handwriting. Wildlife and natural history exhibits, a gift shop, and a good café are also here. ⊠ *Hwy. 7, Garrison Savannah,* ☎ *246/427–0201.* ⊡ *Bds$10.* ☉ *Mon.–Sat. 9–5, Sun. 2–6.*

❼ The Careenage. The finger of sea that made early Bridgetown a natural harbor and a gathering place is where working schooners were careened (turned on their sides) to be scraped of barnacles and repainted. Today the Careenage serves mainly as a berth for pleasure yachts and charter boats. The two bridges over the Careenage are the Chamberlain Bridge and the Charles O'Neal Bridge.

❹ Harry Bayley Observatory. Built in 1963, this is the headquarters of the Barbados Astronomical Society. The observatory, equipped with a 14-inch reflector telescope, is rather unique in the Caribbean. ⊠ *Off Hwy. 6, Clapham,* ☎ *246/426–1317 or 246/422–2394.* ⊡ *$4.* ☉ *Fri. 8:30 AM–11:30 PM.*

❶ Jewish Synagogue. This is the oldest synagogue in the Western Hemisphere. The original building, dating from 1654, was destroyed in a hurricane. It was rebuilt in 1833 and has recently been restored. The synagogue holds services and is a Barbados National Trust building. ⊠ *Synagogue La.,* ☎ *246/426–5792.* ☉ *Weekdays 9–4.*

❺ Parliament Buildings. Built around 1870, these buildings, adjacent to Trafalgar Square, house the third oldest Parliament of the British Commonwealth. A series of stained-glass windows depicting British monarchs from James I to Queen Victoria adorn these Victorian government buildings. Like so many smaller buildings in Bridgetown, they stand beside a growing number of modern offices.

❷ Queen's Park. Northeast of Bridgetown, Queen's Park has one of the largest trees in Barbados, an immense baobab more than 10 centuries old. The historic Queen's Park House, former home of the commander of the British troops, has been converted into a theater, with an exhibition room on the lower floor and a restaurant. ☉ *Daily 9–5.*

58

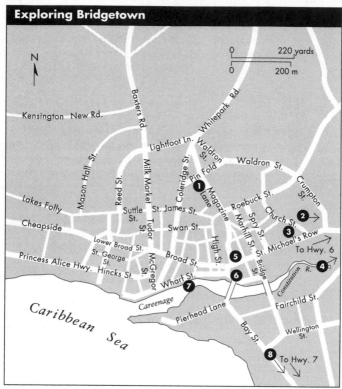

Barbados
Museum, **8**

The Careenage, **7**

Harry Bayley
Observatory, **4**

Jewish
Synagogue, **1**

Parliament
Buildings, **5**

Queen's Park, **2**

St. Michael's
Cathedral, **3**

Trafalgar
Square, **6**

3 **St. Michael's Cathedral.** Although no one has proved it conclusively, George Washington, on his only visit outside the United States, is said to have worshiped at St. Michael's Cathedral, east of Trafalgar Square. The structure was built between 1784 and 1786 and survived the 1831 hurricane that devastated much of Barbados.

6 **Trafalgar Square.** In the center of town, across from the Parliament Buildings and the Careenage, this monument to Lord Horatio Nelson predates Nelson's Column in London's Trafalgar Square by 27 years. Nelson was based in Barbados as a 19-year-old lieutenant in 1777, and did not leave until 1805, a few months before the battle of Trafalgar.

The West Coast

Speightstown and Holetown are the island's other major towns (after Bridgetown, the capital). Holetown is the center of the Gold Coast resort area and the place where Captain John Powell landed in 1625 and claimed the island in the name of King James. The town was originally called Jamestown, until the off-loading and cleaning of ships in its small channel created such filthy conditions that the area was dubbed The Hole. The channel isn't used for these purposes anymore and the name has regained some dignity with the addition of "town". The port city of Speightstown is more characteristically West Indian with its 19th-century architecture (many of the buildings have been restored or are undergoing work) and quaint shops and restaurants. The natural history of Barbados is also represented in the central parishes by fascinating caves, a mile-long gully, and beautiful tropical vegetation.

Numbers in the margin correspond to points of interest on the Exploring Barbados map.

Sights to See

10 **Emancipation Memorial.** This larger-than-life statue of a slave—with raised hands, evoking both contempt and victory, and broken chains hanging from each wrist—is commonly referred to as the "Bussa Statue." Bussa was the man who, in the early part of the 19th century, led the first slave rebellion in Barbados. The statue's location at the St. Barnabas Roundabout (intersection of the ABC Highway and

Exploring Barbados

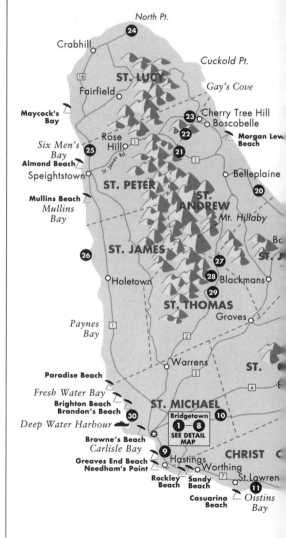

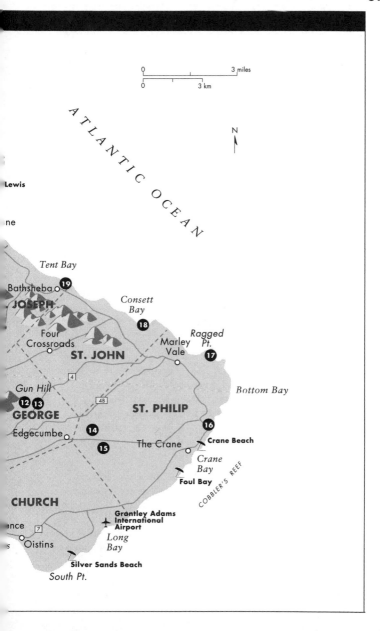

0   3 miles

0   3 km

N

A T L A N T I C   O C E A N

Lewis

ne

Tent Bay

Bathsheba ○ **19**

JOSEPH

Consett Bay

18

Four
Crossroads ○

ST. JOHN

Ragged Pt.

Marley
Vale ○

17

4

4B

Gun Hill

Bottom Bay

12 13

GEORGE

ST. PHILIP

Edgecumbe ○

14

16

15

The Crane ○

Crane Beach

Crane Bay

Foul Bay

COBBLER'S REEF

CHURCH

7

ence

○ Oistins

s

**Grantley Adams
International
Airport**

*Long
Bay*

Silver Sands Beach

South Pt.

Highway 5, St. Michael), overlooking a broad expanse of cane field, makes the monument all the more moving.

㉗ Flower Forest. Enjoy meandering through 8 acres of fragrant flowering bushes, canna and ginger lilies, puffball trees, and more than a hundred other species of flora in a tranquil setting. From this area, you can also have a beautiful view of Mt. Hillaby. ⊠ *Richmond Plantation, Hwy. 2, St. Joseph,* ☎ *246/433–8152.* ☜ *$6.* ☉ *Daily 9–5.*

☾ ㉖ Folkestone Marine Park & Visitor Centre. On land and off there's a lot to enjoy here: A museum illuminates some of the island's marine life; and for some firsthand viewing, there's an underwater snorkeling trail around Dottin's Reef (glass-bottom boats are available for nonswimmers). A dredge barge sunk in shallow water is home to myriad fish, and it and the reef are popular with scuba divers. Also keep your eyes out for huge sea fans, soft coral, and the occasional giant turtle.⊠ *Holetown, St. James,* ☎ *246/422–2314.* ☜ *50¢. Closed Mon.*

⑫ Francia Plantation House. Owned and occupied by descendants of the original owner, the house was built in 1913 in a style that blends European and Caribbean influences. You can tour the house and gardens. ⊠ *St. George,* ☎ *246/429-0474.* ☜ *$1.50.* ☉ *Weekdays 10–4.*

⑬ Gun Hill Signal Station. The view from Gun Hill is so pretty it seems almost unreal. Shades of green and gold cover the fields all the way to the horizon, the picturesque gun tower is surrounded by brilliant flowers, and the white limestone lion behind the garrison is a famous landmark. Military invalids were once sent here to convalesce. ⊠ *St. George,* ☎ *246/429–1358.* ☜ *$4.* ☉ *Mon.–Sat. 9–5.*

☾ ㉙ Harrison's Cave. This pale-gold limestone cavern, complete with stalactites, stalagmites, subterranean streams, and a 40-ft waterfall, is an unusual find in the Caribbean. The one-hour tours are made by electric tram (hard hats are provided, but all that may fall on you is a little dripping water) and fill up fast, so you may want to reserve a spot ahead of time. ⊠ *Hwy. 2, St. Thomas,* ☎ *246/438–6640.* ☜ *$7.50.* ☉ *Daily 9–6; last tour at 4.*

30 **Mount Gay Rum Visitors Centre.** Take a 45-minute tour to learn the colorful story behind the world's oldest rum and about the rum-making process. The tour concludes with a tasting, and rum can be purchased at the gift shop. You can stay on for lunch if you wish. The center is just five minutes north of the port and downtown Bridgetown. ⊠ *Spring Garden Hwy.,* ☎ *246/425–8757.* 🖃 *$5.* ☉ *Weekdays 9–4.*

28 **Welchman Hall Gully.** Part of the National Trust in St. Thomas, here's another chance to commune with nature. Acres of labeled flowers and trees stretch along in a mile-long natural gully, with the occasional green monkey showing itself and great peace and quiet. ⊠ *St. Thomas,* ☎ *246/438–6671.* 🖃 *$5.* ☉ *Daily 9–5.*

The East Coast

The Atlantic Ocean crashes dramatically against the East Coast of Barbados, where, over eons, the waves have eroded the shoreline into caves, arches, cliffs, and sea rocks that look like giant mushrooms. Narrow roads weave among the ridges, and small villages cling to hillsides that slide into the sea. Local people come to the coastal areas called Bathsheba and Cattlewash to spend weekends and holidays.

Sights to See

★ **19** **Andromeda Gardens.** A fascinating collection of unusual and beautiful plant specimens from around the world are cultivated in 6 acres of gardens nestled among streams, ponds, and rocky outcroppings in the cliffs overlooking the sea above the Bathsheba coastline. The gardens were created in 1954 with flowering plants collected by the late horticulturist Iris Bannochie. They are now administered by the Barbados National Trust. The Hibiscus Café serves snacks and drinks, and there's a Best of Barbados gift shop on the property. ⊠ *Bathsheba, St. Joseph,* ☎ *246/433–9384.* 🖃 *$5.* ☉ *Daily 9–5.*

24 **Animal Flower Cave.** Small sea anemones, or sea worms, resemble jewel-like flowers when they open their tiny tentacles. They live in small pools—some large enough to swim in—in a cave at the northern tip of Barbados. The view from inside the cavern as waves break just outside is

magnificent. ⊠ *North Point, St. Lucy,* ☎ *246/439–8797.*
🎫 *$1.50.* ⊙ *Daily 9–4.*

㉚ Barclays Park. Just north of Bathsheba, this park was given
to the people of Barbados by Barclays Bank to commem-
orate the Independence of Barbados in 1966. It offers a gor-
geous view of the ocean, plus picnic facilities. At the nearby
Chalky Mount Potteries, you'll find potters making and selling their wares.

⑱ Codrington Theological College. The coral-stone buildings
and serenely beautiful grounds of Codrington College, an
Anglican seminary founded in 1745, stand on a cliff overlooking Consett Bay. Visitors are welcome to tour the
buildings and grounds, including a well-laid-out nature
trail. Keep in mind, though, that this is a theological college and beachwear is not appropriate. ⊠ *St. John,* ☎
246/433–1274. 🎫 *$2.50.* ⊙ *Daily 10–4.*

☝ ⑮ Rum Factory and Heritage Park. A long entrance through
the cane fields brings you to the first rum distillery to be
built in Barbados in this century. Opened in late 1996 on
a 350-year-old molasses and sugar plantation, the spotless,
high-tech distillery produces ESA Field white rum and its
premium Alleyne Arthur varieties. Adjacent is the 7-acre
Heritage Park, which showcases Bajan skills and talents in
its Art Foundry and Cane Pit Amphitheatre, along with an
array of shops and carts filled exclusively with local products, crafts, and foods. ⊠ *Foursquare Plantation, St. Philip,*
☎ *246/423–6669.* 🎫 *$12.* ⊙ *Sun.–Thurs. 9–5, Fri.–Sat.
9–9.*

⑭ Sunbury Plantation House & Museum. Lovingly rebuilt
after a 1995 fire destroyed everything but the 2½-ft-thick
flint-and-stone walls of this 300-year-old plantation house,
Sunbury is once again an elegant representation of life on
a Barbadian sugar estate in the 18th and 19th centuries.
Period furniture has been donated to lend an air of au-
thenticity. Plan to come for lunch (☞ Chapter 3). ⊠ *St.
Philip,* ☎ *246/423–6270.* 🎫 *$5 tour only; $12.50 with
buffet lunch.* ⊙ *Daily 10–5.*

Northern Barbados

The northern reaches of the island, St. Peter and St. Lucy parishes, provide a range of terrain. Between the tiny fishing towns along the northwestern coast and the sweeping views out to the Atlantic Ocean on the northeastern coast are forest and farm, moor and mountain. Most guides include this loop on a daylong island tour—it's a beautiful drive.

Sights to See

🦎 ② **Barbados Wildlife Reserve.** The reserve is home to herons, land turtles, a kangaroo, screeching peacocks, innumerable green monkeys, geese, brilliantly colored parrots, and a friendly otter. The fauna are not in cages, so step carefully and keep your hands to yourself. The preserve has been much improved in recent years with the addition of a giant walk-in aviary and natural-history exhibits. Terrific photo opportunities are everywhere. ✉ *Farley Hill, St. Peter,* ☎ *246/422–8826.* 🎫 *$10.* ⊙ *Daily 10–5.*

② **Farley Hill.** At this national park in northern St. Peter, across the road from the Barbados Wildlife Reserve, the imposing ruins of a once-magnificent plantation great house are surrounded by gardens, lawns, an avenue of towering royal palms, and gigantic mahogany, whitewood, and casuarina trees. Partially rebuilt for the filming of *Island in the Sun,* the 1957 film starring Harry Belafonte and Dorothy Dandridge, the structure was later destroyed by fire. Behind the estate, there's a sweeping view of the part of Barbados called Scotland for its rugged landscape. ✉ *St. Peter.* 🎫 *$1.50 per car; walkers free.* ⊙ *Daily 8:30–6.*

② **St. Nicholas Abbey.** This property was named for a former owner, a prominent farmer with no religious connection to St. Nicholas. It is the oldest (circa 1650) great house in Barbados and is worth visiting for its stone-and-wood architecture—one of only three original Jacobean-style houses still standing in the Western Hemisphere. It has Dutch gables, finials of coral stone, and an herb garden in a medieval design. Fascinating home movies by the present owner's father record Bajan town and plantation life in the 1930s. ✉ *Near Cherry Tree Hill, St. Lucy,* ☎ *246/422–8725.* 🎫 *$2.50.* ⊙ *Weekdays 10–3:30.*

㉕ Six Men's Bay. On the northwest coast, on Highway 1 beyond Speightstown, a winding road takes you through tiny fishing and boat-building villages in what is truly picture-postcard Barbados—a far cry from the tourist areas.

The South Coast

The heavily traveled south coast of Christ Church is much more built up than the St. James Parish coast in the west. Here you'll find St. Lawrence Gap, with its condos, high-rise hotels, beach parks, many places to eat and shop, and the traffic (including public transportation) that serves them.

Many chattel houses, the property of tenant farmers and typically Barbadian in style, are farther to the southwest. These ever-expandable houses were built to be dismantled and moved when necessary.

Sights to See

❾ George Washington House. In 1751, long before the American Revolution, George Washington brought his brother Lawrence to Barbados to recover from tuberculosis. At this house at the top of Bush Hill, in the historic Garrison area south of Bridgetown, the brothers spent seven weeks, during which time poor George contracted smallpox (it was his only trip abroad). The house has been converted to offices, and is easily identified by the coral-stone windmill in the parking lot.

⓫ Oistins. The major town along the South Coast of Barbados, Oistins is a fishing area where boats leave before dawn each morning and return to the waterfront fish market with their catches. The annual Oistins Fish Festival, held at the end of March, is a weekend of celebration, boat racing, arts and crafts, dancing, and singing.

⓱ Ragged Point Lighthouse. Appropriately named, this is where the sun first shines on Barbados and its dramatic Atlantic seascape. You can see the entire east coast from the lighthouse—a particularly fascinating view on a stormy day.

⓰ Sam Lord's Castle. The Regency house built by the buccaneer Sam Lord is considered by many to be the finest mansion in Barbados. Built in 1820 and now part of a resort

(☞ Chapter 2), the opulent estate features double verandas on all sides and magnificent plaster ceilings created by Charles Rutter, who crafted the ceilings in England's Windsor Castle. Most of the rooms are furnished with the fine mahogany furniture and gilt mirrors Sam Lord is reputed to have acquired from passing ships that he lured onto treacherous reefs by hanging lanterns in palm trees to simulate harbor lights. ⊠ *Long Bay, St. Philip,* ☎ *246/423–7350.* ⬚ *$5; hotel guests free.* ⊙ *Daily 10–4.*

Guided Tours

A half- or full-day **bus** or **taxi tour** is a good way to get your bearings and can be arranged by your hotel. The price varies according to the number of attractions included; an average full-day tour (five–six hours) costs about $30–$50 per person and generally includes lunch and admissions.

Bajan Helicopters (⊠ Bridgetown Heliport, ☎ 246/431–0069) offers an eagle's-eye view of Barbados. Price per person ranges from $65 for a 20- to 25-minute "Discover Barbados" tour to $115 for a 30- to 35-minute full "Island Tour".

Every Wednesday afternoon from mid-January through mid-April, the **Barbados National Trust** (☎ 246/436–9033 or 246/426–2421) offers a bus tour of historical great houses and modern private homes open for public viewing. The cost is $17.50 per person, which includes admissions to the houses and transportation to and from your hotel.

Highland Outdoor Tours (⊠ Canefield, St. Thomas, ☎ 246/438–8069) specializes in adventure trips to the island's seldom-seen natural wonders. You have the option of half-day or full-day horseback treks (including a bareback ride in the surf), scenic hiking expeditions, or tractor-drawn jitney rides through some of Barbados's great plantations. Prices range from $25 per person for a short, two-hour plantation tour by open jitney to $100 per person for the 7-mi Horseback Trek. A 5-mi Scenic Safari Hike is $70. All tours include refreshments and transportation to and from your hotel.

Mystic Mountain Bike Tours (⊠ Prospect, St. James, ☎ 246/424–4730) takes riders of all abilities on half- and full-day guided mountain-bike excursions. Bikes, equipment, hotel transfers, lunch and refreshments, and a support vehicle are provided. Prices begin at $47.50.

L. E. Williams Tour Co. (☎ 246/427–1043) offers an 80-mi island tour for about $50. A bus picks you up between 8:30 AM and 9:30 AM and takes you through Bridgetown, the St. James beach area, past the Animal Flower Cave, Farley Hill, Cherry Tree Hill, Morgan Lewis Mill, the East Coast, St. John's Church, Sam Lord's Castle, and Oistin's fishing village, and to the parish of St. Michael. Drinks are served along the way, and there's a stop at the Atlantis Hotel in Bathsheba for a West Indian lunch.

Sally Shearn operates **VIP Tour Services** (⊠ Hillcrest Villa, Upton, St. Michael, ☎ 246/429–4617), which creates tours to suit your taste. Bajan-born Ms. Shearn knows her island well and provides a swim at her favorite beach. She picks you up in an air-conditioned Mercedes-Benz and charges $40 per hour for four people, with a minimum of four hours.

9 Cruising to Barbados

CHOOSING YOUR CRUISE

The right ship is one that makes you comfortable. Every ship has its own personality, depending upon its size, when it was built, and its purpose. Big ships are more stable and offer a huge variety of activities and facilities. Smaller ships feel intimate, like private clubs. Each type of ship satisfies a certain type of passenger, and for every big-ship fan there is somebody who would never set foot aboard one of these "floating resorts."

But when choosing your cruise, the size of the ship isn't the only factor to consider. You also need to find out about the nature of the experience you will have—the lifestyle and activities available by day and after dark, the mealtime hours and dining-room dress codes, how roomy the ship is, and how good the service is apt to be. Equally important are your itinerary, the accommodations, and the cost of the cruise.

Types of Ships

Although all ocean liners are equipped with swimming pools, spas, nightclubs, theaters, and casinos, there are three distinct types: classic liners, cruise liners, and mega-ships. Many **classic liners,** ships constructed between 1950 and 1969 for transatlantic or other ocean crossings, are still sailing in the fleets of many cruise lines. Beginning in the 1960s, ship lines began to create vessels specifically for cruising. Some of these **cruise liners** were brand new; others were converted ferries or freighters. Vessels known as **megaships,** the biggest cruise ships ever built, first appeared in the late 1980s and, with their immense proportions and passenger capacities, immediately established a new standard of cruise-ship design.

Classic Liners

With their long, sweeping hulls and stepped-back passenger decks, these vessels defined passenger-ship design for decades. Now serving cruise duty, they were originally configured to keep passengers happy during long ocean cross-

Pick up
the phone.

Pick up
the miles.

Calling Card

415 555 1234 2244
J.D. SMITH

WorldPhone

Use your MCI Card® to make an international call from virtually anywhere in the world and earn frequent flyer miles on one of seven major airlines.

Enroll in an MCI Airline Partner Program today. In the U.S., call **1-800-FLY-FREE**. Overseas, call MCI collect at **1-916-567-5151**.

1. To use your MCI Card, just dial the WorldPhone access number of the country you're calling from.
   (For a complete listing of codes, visit www.mci.com.)
2. Dial or give the operator your MCI Card number.
3. Dial or give the number you're calling.

# American Samoa	633-2MCI (633-2624)	# Guyana	177
# Antigua (Available from public card phones only)	#2	# Haiti (CC) ÷	193
# Argentina (CC)	0800-5-1002	Haiti IIIC Access in French/Creole	190
# Aruba ÷	800-888-8	Honduras ÷	122
# Bahamas	1-800-888-8000	# Jamaica ÷	1-800-888-8000
# Barbados	1-800-888-8000	(From Special Hotels only)	873
# Belize	557 from hotels	# Mexico	
	815 from pay phones	Avantel (CC)	91-800-021-8000
# Bermuda ÷	1-800-888-8000	Telmex ▲	95-800-674-7000
# Bolivia ♦	0-800-2222	Mexico IIIC Access	91-800-021-1000
# Brazil (CC)	000-8012	# Netherlands Antilles (CC) ÷	001-800-888-8000
# British Virgin Islands ÷	1-800-888-8000	Nicaragua (CC)	166
# Cayman Islands	1-800-888-8000	(Outside of Managua, dial 02 first)	
# Chile (CC)		Nicaragua IIIC Access in Spanish	★2 from any
To call using CTC ■	800-207-300		public pay phone
To call using ENTEL ■	800-360-180	# Panama	108
# Colombia (CC) ♦	980-16-0001	Military Bases	2810-108
Columbia IIIC Access in Spanish	980-16-1000	# Paraguay ÷	008-112-800
# Costa Rica ♦	0800-012-2222	# Peru	0-800-500-10
# Dominica	1-800-888-8000	# Puerto Rico (CC)	1-800-888-8000
# Dominican Republic (CC) ÷	1-800-888-8000	# St. Lucia ÷	1-800-888-8000
Dominican Republic IIIC Access in Spanish	1121	# Trinidad & Tobago ÷	1-800-888-8000
# Ecuador (CC) ÷	999-170	# Turks & Caicos ÷	1-800-888-8000
El Salvador ♦	800-1767	# Uruguay	000-412
# Grenada ÷	1-800-888-8000	# U.S. Virgin Islands (CC)	1-800-888-8000
Guatemala (CC) ♦	9999-189	# Venezuela (CC) ÷ ♦	800-1114-0

Is this a great time, or what? :-)

ings. Typically, their cabins and closets are larger than those on vessels built for cruising. Deck space is sheltered, with fully or partially enclosed promenades that allow you to relax on deck even during foul weather. A few are still steam powered, without the vibrations sometimes associated with diesel power. Rich wood panels the walls, and fixtures may be the original brass. Smaller ships may feel cramped because of low ceilings in the lobby and corridors. But on the most opulent vessels, public spaces designed to inspire still do. There are balconies above the dining room, where musicians can serenade diners; stained glass graces the cinemas and other public spaces; and grand staircases lead from one deck to another. Such traditional features have proved so enduring they have been incorporated in the plans for some of today's newest vessels.

Although classic ships typically carry between 600 and 1,000 passengers and register between 20,000 and 30,000 tons, a couple of them are among the largest passenger ships afloat.

Cruise Liners

When shipbuilders stopped constructing vessels for transportation and started designing them for vacationing, the cruise liner entered the scene. On these ships, outdoor deck space is plentiful; stateroom space is not. Many have a wraparound outdoor promenade deck that allows you to stroll or jog the perimeter of the ship. Older cruise liners resemble the transatlantic ships from which they are descended: Decks are stacked one atop the other in steps, and the hull amidships may appear to droop, so the bow and stern seem to curve upward. In the newest cruise liners, traditional meets trendy. You find atrium lobbies and expansive sun and sports decks, picture windows instead of portholes, and cabins that open onto private verandas. The smallest cruise liners carry 500 passengers and are no bigger than 10,000 tons, while the largest accommodate 1,500 passengers, exceed 50,000 tons, and are stuffed with diversions—almost like megaships.

Megaships

The centerpiece of most megaships is a three-, five-, or seven-story central atrium. However, these giant vessels are most easily recognized by their boxy profile: The hull and superstructure rise straight out of the water, as many as 14 stories tall, topped out by a huge sun or sports deck with a jogging track and swimming pool, which may be Olympic size. Some megaships, but not all, also have a wraparound promenade deck. Like the latest cruise liners, picture windows are standard equipment, and cabins in the top categories have private verandas. From their casinos and discos to their fitness centers, everything is proportionally bigger and more extravagant than on other ships. Between 1,500 and 2,500 passengers can be accommodated, and tonnage ranges from 60,000 to 70,000 or more.

Cruise Yachts

At the opposite end of the spectrum from the megaship is the tiny cruise yacht. These intimate vessels carry from 100 to 300 passengers, register between 4,000 and 15,000 tons, and are like miniature ocean liners, with big-ship amenities such as fitness centers, casinos, lounges, and swimming pools. What sets these yachts apart from typical ocean liners is that passengers are treated like royalty. Cabins are all outside suites equipped with every creature comfort on the high seas—from VCRs and stocked mini-bars to marble baths. Built into the stern of some of these vessels are retractable platforms, which are lowered for water sports when the ship is at anchor in calm waters.

Motor-Sail Vessels

A number of cruise vessels were designed as sailing ships. With their sails unfurled, they are an impressive sight. But since they must keep to a schedule, they cannot rely solely on wind power. So all are equipped with engines as well. Usually they employ both means of propulsion, a technique known as motor sailing, to put on a good show and make the next port on time. These vessels range from small wind-jammers carrying a handful of passengers to rather large clipper-style ships that approach the size of a small ocean liner and accommodate almost 400 passengers.

The Cruise Experience

Your cruise experience will be shaped by several factors, and to determine whether a particular ship's style will suit you, you need to do a bit of research. Is a full program of organized activities scheduled by day? What happens in the evening? Are there one or two seatings in the dining room? If there is more than one, you will not be allowed to arrive and exit as the spirit moves you but instead must show up promptly when service begins—and clear out within a specified time. What kind of entertainment is offered after dark? And how often do passengers dress up for dinner? Some cruises are fancier than others.

Although no two cruises are quite the same, even aboard the same ship, the cruise experience tends to fall into three categories.

Formal

Formal cruises embody the ceremony of cruising. Generally available on ocean liners and cruise yachts sailing for seven days or longer, formal cruises recall the days when traveling by ship was an event in itself. By day, shipboard lifestyle is generally unstructured, with few organized activities. Tea and bouillon may be served to the accompaniment of music from a classical trio in the afternoon. Ashore, passengers may be treated to a champagne beach party. Meals in the dining room are served in a single seating, and passengers are treated to the finest cuisine afloat. Jackets and ties for men are the rule for dinner, tuxedos are not uncommon, and the dress code is observed faithfully throughout the evening. Pianists, cabaret acts, and local entertainers provide nighttime diversion. Service is extremely attentive and personalized. Passenger-to-crew and space ratios are best. Because these cruises tend to attract destination-oriented passengers, shore excursions—such as private museum tours—sometimes are included in the fare, as are pre- or post-cruise land packages and sometimes even tips.

Semiformal

Semiformal cruises are a bit more relaxed than their formal counterparts. Meals are served in two seatings on ocean liners or one seating on specialty ships, menu choices are plentiful, and the cuisine is on a par with that available in better restaurants. Men tend to wear a jacket and tie to dinner most nights. Adding a distinct flair to the dining room is the common practice of staffing the restaurant with waiters of one nationality. Featured dishes may be prepared table side, and you often are able, with advance notice, to order a special diet, such as kosher, low-salt, low-cholesterol, sugar free, or vegetarian. There is a daily program of scheduled events, but there's time for more independent pursuits; passengers with similar interests are often encouraged to meet at appointed times for chess or checkers, deck games, and other friendly contests. Production-style shows are staged each evening, but the disco scene may not be too lively. Passenger-to-crew and space ratios assure good service and plenty of room for each passenger. Look for semiformal cruises aboard classic liners, cruise liners, megaships, and a few expedition ships on voyages of seven days or longer.

Casual

Casual cruises are the most popular. Shipboard dress and lifestyle are informal. Meals in the dining room are served in two seatings on ocean liners and one seating on specialty ships; menus are usually not extensive, and the food is good but not extraordinary; your options may be limited if you have special dietetic requirements. Men dress in sport shirts and slacks for dinner most nights, in jackets and ties only two or three evenings of a typical seven-day sailing. Aboard casual ocean liners, activities are more diverse than on formal and semiformal ships, and there is almost always something going on, from bingo to beer-chugging contests. Las Vegas–style variety shows or Broadway revues headline the evening entertainment. Discos bop into the wee hours. Passenger-to-crew and space ratios are generally good, but service tends to be less personal.

Look for casual cruises aboard classic liners, cruise liners, and megaships sailing three- to seven-day itineraries to fun-and-sun destinations; expedition ships; motor-sailing ships; riverboats; and coastal cruisers calling on more unusual ports.

Theme Cruises

These increasingly popular sailings highlight a particular activity or topic. Onboard lectures and other events are coordinated with shoreside excursions. There are photography cruises, square-dancing cruises, sports cruises, financial-planning cruises, wine-tasting cruises, and more. The most popular destinations for theme cruises are Alaska and the Caribbean. To find out about theme cruises that might interest you, consult with the individual cruise lines or a travel agent. Lines that offer the greatest variety of theme cruises are **American Hawaii Cruises, Cunard Line, Dolphin Cruise Line, Holland America Line, Majesty Cruise Line, Norwegian Cruise Line, Premier Cruise Lines,** and **Royal Caribbean Cruise Line.**

Of the major cruise-only agencies, one of the best to contact for theme cruises is CruiseMasters (☞ Agencies to Contact *in* Booking Your Cruise, *below*). For a music cruise, contact tour operators Dailey-Thorp Travel (⊠ 330 W. 58th St., Suite 610, New York, NY 10019, ☎ 212/307–1555, FAX 212/974–1420).

Ship Itineraries

In choosing the best cruise for you, a ship's itinerary is another important factor. The length of the cruise will determine the variety and number of ports you visit, but so will the type of itinerary and the point of departure. Some cruises, known as **loop cruises,** start and end at the same point and usually explore ports close to one another; **one-way cruises** start at one port and end at another and range farther afield.

Most cruises to the Caribbean are loop cruises. You often have a choice of departure points. Sailings out of San Juan, Puerto Rico, can visit up to six ports in seven days, while loop cruises out of Florida can reach up to four ports in the same time.

BOOKING YOUR CRUISE

Getting the Best Cruise for Your Dollar

It's best to pick your vessel and itinerary first, and then try to get the best price. Like everything in retail, each cruise has a brochure list price. But like the sticker price on a new car, nobody actually pays this amount. These days, if you asked any 10 cruise passengers on any given ship what they paid, they would give you 10 different answers. Discounts from cruise lines and agencies can range from 5% on a single fare to 50% on the second fare in a cabin.

Approach deep discounts with skepticism. Fewer than a dozen cabins may be offered at the discounted price, they may be inside cabins, and the fare may not include air transportation or transfers between the airport and the ship. Finally, do the math. A promotion might sound catchy, but if you divide the price by the number of days you'll be cruising and include the cost of air and accommodations, you might find that the deal of the century is really a dud.

Deals and Discounts

EARLY-BIRD SPECIALS

Almost all cruise lines provide a discount for passengers who book and put down a deposit far in advance; an additional discount may be provided if payment is made in full at the time of booking. These discounts, given to passengers who book at least six months before departure, range from 10% to 50% off the brochure rate. (Brochures are usually issued a year or more in advance of sailing dates.) Most early-booking discounts in the Caribbean include round-trip air-fare. Booking a popular cruise early is the best way to get the best price; there will likely be no last-minute deals on these sailings. The other advantage of booking far in advance is that you're more likely to get the cabin and meal seating you want. On most cruises, the cheapest and most expensive cabins sell out first.

LAST-MINUTE SAVINGS

In recent years, cruise lines have provided fewer and fewer last-minute deals. However, if a particular cruise is not selling well, a cruise line may pick certain large cruise-only travel agencies to unload unsold cabins. These deals, sometimes referred to by agents as "distressed merchandise," are typically available three weeks to three months before the cruise departs. These specials are unadvertised, but may be listed in the agencies' newsletters and on their cruise telephone hot lines (☞ Agencies to Contact, *below*). Keep in mind that your choice of cabin and meal seating is limited for such last-minute deals. Distressed merchandise on older ships, those built before the 1980s, may be limited to smaller cabins in undesirable areas of the ship. Last-minute deals may only be available in certain regions.

Using a Travel Agent

Since nearly all cruises are sold through travel agents, the agent you choose to work with can be just as important as the ship you sail on. The most qualified agents are members of CLIA (Cruise Lines International Association). Agents who are CLIA Accredited Cruise Counsellors or Master Cruise Counsellors have had extensive cruise and ship inspection experience. If you opt for a cruise-only agency (☞ *below*), they should also be a member of NACOA (National Association of Cruise-Only Agencies). These agents are also experienced cruisers. Finally, the most reputable agencies, both full-service and cruise-only, are members of ASTA (American Society of Travel Agents).

The top agencies can more or less get you the same price on most cruises, because they'll guarantee that if the cruise line lowers the price in a promotion, you'll get the better deal. So look for an agency that offers this guarantee. But the overall value of your cruise depends on an agency's service, and agencies that are willing to go the extra mile for their clients by providing free cruise-discount newsletters, cabin upgrades, dollar-stretching advice, and 24-hour service in case of a problem are your best bet.

Cruise-Only Travel Agents

As the name implies, "cruise-only" travel agencies specialize in selling cruises. However, these agencies can sell you air tickets and other travel arrangements, too, as part of your cruise package. Sometimes, your choice may be limited to a package put together by the cruise line. Increasingly, though, cruise-only agencies are putting together their own custom-designed cruise vacations.

Full-Service Travel Agents

Full-service agents have broad travel experience, but may be less knowledgeable about cruise lines than their cruise-only counterparts. If you know exactly what line and ship you want to sail on and are more concerned about your pre- or post-cruise land arrangements, a full-service agent may be more helpful. (But keep in mind that full-service agencies may not have the same discounts as cruise-only agencies.) If you choose to use a full-service agency, look for one that has a "cruise" desk with agents who sell only cruises. Then, you get the best of both worlds.

Spotting Swindlers

Always be on the lookout for a scam. Although reputable agencies far outnumber crooks, a handful of marketeers use deceptive and unethical tactics. The best way to avoid being fleeced is to pay for your cruise with a credit card, from deposit to full payment. That way, if an agency goes out of business before your cruise departs, you can cancel payment on services not rendered. Two tip-offs that an agency may be a bad apple: It doesn't accept credit cards and it asks for a deposit that is more than what the cruise line has requested (check the brochure). To avoid a disreputable agency, make sure the one you choose has been in business for at least five years. Check its reputation with the local Better Business Bureau or consumer protection agency *before* you pay any deposits. If a cruise price seems too good to be true, it could mean the agency is desperate to bring in money and may close its doors tomorrow, so don't be tempted by agencies that claim they can beat any price. Be wary of bait-and-switch tactics: If you're told that an advertised bargain cruise is sold out, don't be persuaded to book a more expensive substitute. Also, if you're told that your cruise reservation was canceled because of overbooking and that you must pay extra for a confirmed rescheduled sailing, demand a full refund. Finally, if ever you fail to receive a voucher or ticket on the promised date, place an inquiry immediately.

Agencies to Contact

The agencies listed below specialize in booking cruises, have been in business at least five years, and emphasize customer service as well as price.

CRUISE ONLY

Cruise Fairs of America (✉ 2029 Century Park E, Suite 950, Los Angeles, CA 90067, ☎ 310/556–2925 or 800/456–4386, FAX 310/556–2254), established in 1987, has a faxback service for information on the latest deals. The agency also publishes a free twice-yearly newsletter with tips on cruising. Cruise Fairs can make independent hotel and air arrangements for a complete cruise vacation.

Cruise Holidays of Kansas City (✉ 7000 N.W. Prairie View Rd., Kansas City, MO 64151, ☎ 816/741–7417 or 800/869–6806, FAX 816/741–7123), a franchisee of Cruise Holidays, a cruise-only agency with outlets throughout the United States, has been in business since 1988. The agency mails out a free newsletter to clients every other month with listings of cruise bargains.

Cruise Line, Inc. (✉ 150 N.W. 168th St., N. Miami Beach, FL 33169, ☎ 305/653–6111 or 800/777–0707, FAX 305/653–6228), established in 1983, publishes *World of Cruising* magazine three times a year and a number of free brochures, including "Guide to First Time Cruising," "Guide to Family Cruises," and "Guide to Cruise Ship Weddings and Honeymoons." The agency has a 24-hour hot line with prerecorded cruise deals that are updated weekly.

Cruise Pro (✉ 2527 E. Thousand Oaks Blvd., Thousand Oaks, CA 91362, ☎ 805/371–9884 or 800/222–7447; 800/258–7447 in CA; FAX 805/371–9084), established in 1983, has special discounts listed in its two-times-per-month mailings to members of its Voyager's Club ($15 to join).

CruiseMasters (✉ 300 Corporate Pointe, Suite 100, Culver City, CA 90230, ☎ 310/568–2040 or 800/242–9000, FAX 310/568–2044), established in 1987, gives each passenger a personalized, bound guide to their ship's ports of call. The guides provide money-saving tips and advice on whether to opt for a prepackaged port excursion or strike out on your own. The agency's Family Cruise Club serves parents cruising with their children. A World Cruise Desk is dedicated to booking very long cruises. CruiseMasters also specializes in theme cruises.

Cruises, Inc. (✉ 5000 Campuswood Dr., E. Syracuse, NY 10357, ☎ 315/463–9695 or 800/854–0500, FAX 315/434–9175) opened its doors in 1981 and now has nearly 200 cruise consultants, including many CLIA Master Cruise Counsellors and Accredited Cruise Counselors. Services provided by the agency include complimentary accident insurance for up to $250,000 per cruise, a monthly bargain bulletin ($19 a yr), and a free twice-a-year cruise directory with cruise reviews, tips, and discounts.

Cruises of Distinction (⊠ 2750 S. Woodward Ave., Bloomfield Hills, MI 48304, ☎ 810/332–2020 or 800/634–3445, FAX 810/333–9743), established in 1984, publishes a free 80-page cruise catalog four times a year. For a fee of $39, which is credited to your first cruise booking, you can receive notification of unadvertised specials by mail or fax.

Don Ton Cruise Tours (⊠ 3151 Airway Ave., E–1, Costa Mesa, CA 92626, ☎ 714/545–3737 or 800/318–1818, FAX 714/545–5275), established in 1972, features a variety of special-interest clubs, including a short-notice club, singles club, family cruise club, and adventure cruise club. The agency is also experienced in personalized pre- and post-cruise land arrangements.

Golden Bear Travel (⊠ 16 Digital Dr., Novato, CA 94949, ☎ 415/382–8900; 800/551–1000 outside CA; FAX 415/382–9086) acts as general sales agent for a number of foreign cruise ships and specializes in longer, luxury cruises. Its Cruise Value club sends members free twice-a-month mailings with special prices on "distressed merchandise" cruises that are not selling well. The agency's Mariner Club runs escorted cruises for passengers who would like to travel as part of a group.

Kelly Cruises (⊠ 1315 W. 22nd St., Suite 105, Oak Brook, IL 60521, ☎ 630/990–1111 or 800/837–7447, FAX 630/990–1147), established in 1986, publishes a quarterly newsletter highlighting new ships and special rates. Passengers can put their name on a free mailing list for last-minute deals. Kelly Cruises also has a new division, Alaska Cruise and Tour Headquarters.

National Discount Cruise Co. (⊠ 1409 N. Cedar Crest Blvd., Allentown, PA 18104, ☎ 610/439–4883 or 800/788–8108, FAX 610/439–8086) is a five-year-old cruise division launched by GTA Travel, an American Express representative that has served travelers since 1967. The cruise division specializes in high-end cruises and includes shipboard credits, exclusive to American Express, on most of the sailings it books. A three-times-a-year newsletter highlights the agency's latest discounts.

Ship 'N' Shore Cruises (⊠ 3650 S. McCall Rd., Engle-
wood, FL 34224, ☎ 941/475–5414 or 800/444–5414, FAX
941/475–1469), an American Express representative
founded in 1987, specializes in affordable Alaska cruise-
tours. The agency has its own fleet of motor coaches and
custom designs its land tours to complement the cruise
itineraries of Alaska's major cruise lines.

Vacations at Sea (⊠ 4919 Canal St., New Orleans, LA
70119, ☎ 504/482–1572 or 800/749–4950, FAX 504/486–
8360), established in 1983, puts together its own pre- and
post-cruise land packages and escorted land tours. The
agency also publishes a free six-times-a-year newsletter
with cruise reviews and discounts.

FULL SERVICE

Ambassador Tours (⊠ 120 Montgomery St., Suite 400, San
Francisco, CA 94104, ☎ 415/981–5678 or 800/989–
9000, FAX 415/982–3490), established in 1955, does 80%
of its business in cruises. Three times a year, the agency dis-
tributes a free 32-page catalog, which lists discounts on
cruises and land packages, plus free monthly discount
alerts.

Time to Travel (⊠ 582 Market St., San Francisco, CA
94104, ☎ 415/421–3333 or 800/524–3300, FAX 415/421–
4857), established in 1935, does 90% of its business in
cruises. It mails a free listing of cruise discounts to its
clients three to five times a month. Time to Travel specializes in pre- and post-cruise land arrangements and claims
its staff of 19 has been nearly everywhere in the world.

White Travel Service (⊠ 127 Park Rd., West Hartford, CT
06119, ☎ 860/233–2648 or 800/547–4790; 860/236–6176
prerecorded cruise hot line with discount listings; FAX
860/236–6177), founded in 1972, does most of its business in cruises and publishes a free 40-page brochure listing the latest cruise discounts.

What to Pack

Generally speaking, plan on one outfit for every two days
of cruising, especially if your wardrobe contains many in-
terchangeable pieces. Men should pack a dark suit, a

tuxedo, or a white dinner jacket and women should pack one long gown or cocktail dress for every two or three formal evenings on board. Most ships have semiformal evenings, when men should wear a jacket and tie. Ships often have convenient laundry facilities as well. Don't overload your luggage with extra toiletries and sundry items; they are easily available in port and in the ship's gift shop (though usually at a premium price). Soaps, and sometimes shampoos and body lotion, are often placed in your cabin compliments of the cruise line.

Electricity
Most cruise ships use U.S.-type 110V, 60-cycle electricity and grounded plugs, but others employ 220V, 50-cycle current and are fitted with European- or English-type outlets. In that case, to use U.S.-purchased electric appliances on board, you'll need an adapter plug. Unless the appliance is dual-voltage and made for travel, you'll also need a converter.

Luggage
Cruise passengers can bring aboard as much luggage as they like and are restricted only by the amount of closet space in their cabin. If you are flying to your point of embarkation, be aware of the airline's luggage policies. Because luggage is often tossed about and stacked as it is moved between ship and airport, take suitcases that can take abuse.

ARRIVING AND DEPARTING

If you have purchased an air-sea package, you will be met by a cruise-company representative when your plane lands at the port city and then shuttled directly to the ship in buses or minivans. Some cruise lines arrange to transport your luggage between airport and ship—you don't have to hassle with baggage claim at the start of your cruise or with baggage check-in at the end. If you decide not to buy the air-sea package but still plan to fly, ask your travel agent if you can use the ship's transfer bus anyway; if you do, you may be required to purchase a round-trip transfer voucher ($5–$20). Otherwise, you will have to take a taxi to the ship.

If you live close to the port of embarkation, bus transportation may be available. If you are part of a group that
has booked a cruise together, this transportation may be
part of your package. Another option for those who live
close to their point of departure is to drive to the ship. The
major U.S. cruise ports all have parking facilities.

Embarkation

Check-In

On arrival at the dock, you must check in before boarding
your ship. (A handful of smaller cruise ships handle check-
in at the airport.) An officer will collect or stamp your ticket,
inspect or even retain your passport or other official iden-
tification, ask you to fill out a tourist card, check that you
have the correct visas, and collect any unpaid port or departure tax. Seating assignments for the dining room are
often handed out at this time, too. You may also register
your credit card to open a shipboard account, although that
may be done later at the purser's office.

After this you may be required to go through a security check
and to pass your hand baggage through an X-ray inspection. These are the same machines in use at airports, so ask
to have your photographic film inspected visually.

Although it takes only five or 10 minutes per family to check
in, lines are often long, so aim for off-peak hours. The worst
time tends to be immediately after the ship begins boarding; the later it is, the less crowded. For example, if boarding begins at 2 PM and continues until 4:30, try to arrive
after 3:30.

Boarding the Ship

Before you walk up the gangway, the ship's photographer
will probably take your picture; there's no charge unless
you buy the picture (usually $6). On board, stewards may
serve welcome drinks in souvenir glasses—for which you're
usually charged between $3 and $5 cash.

You will either be escorted to your cabin by a steward or,
on a smaller ship, given your key by a ship's officer and directed to your cabin. Some elevators are unavailable to passengers during boarding, since they are used to transport

luggage. You may arrive to find your luggage outside your stateroom or just inside the door; if it doesn't arrive within a half hour before sailing, contact the purser. If you are among the unlucky few whose luggage doesn't make it to the ship in time, the purser will trace it and arrange to have it flown to the next port.

Disembarkation

The last night of your cruise is full of business. On most ships you must place everything except your hand luggage outside your cabin door, ready to be picked up by midnight. Color-coded tags, distributed to your cabin in a debarkation packet, should be placed on your luggage before the crew collects it. Your designated color will later determine when you leave the ship and help you retrieve your luggage on the pier.

Your shipboard bill is left in your room during the last day; to pay the bill (if you haven't already put it on your credit card) or to settle any questions, you must stand in line at the purser's office. Tips to the cabin steward and dining staff are distributed on the last night.

The next morning, in-room breakfast service is usually not available because stewards are too busy. Most passengers clear out of their cabins as soon as possible, gather their hand luggage, and stake out a chair in one of the public lounges to await the ship's clearance through customs. Be patient—it takes a long time to unload and sort thousands of pieces of luggage. Passengers are disembarked by groups according to the color-coded tags placed on luggage the night before; those with the earliest flights get off first. If you have a tight connection, notify the purser before the last day, and he or she may be able to arrange faster preclearing and debarkation for you.

ON BOARD

Checking Out Your Cabin

The first thing to do upon arriving at your cabin or suite is to make sure that everything is in order. If there are two twin beds instead of the double bed you wanted, or other serious problems, ask to be moved *before* the ship departs. Unless the ship is full, you can usually persuade the chief housekeeper or hotel manager to allow you to change cabins. It is customary to tip the stewards who assist you in moving to another cabin.

Since your cabin is your home away from home for a few days or weeks, everything should be to your satisfaction. Take a good look around: Is the cabin clean and orderly? Do the toilet, shower, and faucets work? Check the telephone and television. Again, major problems should be addressed immediately. Minor concerns, such as not enough bath towels or pillows, can wait until the frenzy of embarkation has subsided.

Your dining-time and seating-assignment card may be in your cabin; now is the time to check it and immediately request any changes.

Shipboard Accounts

Virtually all cruise ships operate as cashless societies. Passengers charge onboard purchases and settle their accounts at the end of the cruise with a credit card, traveler's checks, or cash. You can sign for wine at dinner, drinks at the bar, shore excursions, gifts in the shop—virtually any expense you may incur aboard ship. On some lines, an imprint from a major credit card is necessary to open an account. Otherwise, a cash deposit may be required and a positive balance maintained to keep the shipboard account open. Either way, you will want to open a line of credit soon after settling into your cabin if an account was not opened for you at embarkation. This easily can be arranged by visiting the purser's office, located in the central atrium or main lobby.

Tipping

For better or worse, tipping is an integral part of the cruise experience. Most companies pay their cruise staff nominal wages and expect tips to make up the difference. Most cruise lines have recommended tipping guidelines, and on many ships "voluntary" tipping for beverage service has been replaced with a mandatory 15% service charge, which is added to every bar bill. On the other hand, the most expensive luxury lines include tipping in the cruise fare and may prohibit crew members from accepting any additional gratuities. On most small adventure ships, a collection box is placed in the dining room or lounge on the last full day of the cruise, and passengers are encouraged to contribute anonymously.

Dining

The chief meals of the day are served in the main dining room, which on most ships can accommodate only half the passengers at once. So meals are usually served in two sittings—early (or main) and late (or second) seatings—usually from 1½ to 2½ hours apart. Early seating for dinner is generally between 6 and 6:30, late seating between 8 and 8:30.

Most cruise ships have a cafeteria-style restaurant, usually located near the swimming pool, where you can eat lunch and breakfast (dinner is usually served only in the dining room). Many ships provide self-serve coffee or tea in their cafeteria around the clock, as well as buffets at midnight.

Increasingly, ships also have alternative restaurants for ethnic cuisines, such as Italian, Chinese, or Japanese food. These are found mostly on newer vessels, although some older liners have been refitted for alternative dining. Other ships have pizzerias, ice-cream parlors, and caviar or cappuccino bars; there may be an extra charge at these facilities.

Entertainment

On ocean liners, the main entertainment lounge or showroom schedules nightly musical revues, magic acts, comedy performances, and variety shows. Generally, the larger the ship, the bigger and more elaborate the productions. Newer ships—and some older ones as well—sometimes feature multitier seating balconies. During the rest of the day the room is used for group activities, such as shore-excursion talks or bingo games.

Casinos

Once a ship is 12 mi off American shores, it is in international waters and gambling is permitted. (Some "cruises to nowhere," in fact, are little more than sailing casinos.) All ocean liners, as well as many cruise yachts and motor-sailing ships, have casinos. On larger vessels, they usually have poker, baccarat, blackjack, roulette, craps, and slot machines. House stakes are much more modest than those in Las Vegas or Atlantic City. On most ships the maximum bet is $200; some ships allow $500. Payouts on the slot machines (some of which take as little as a nickel) are generally much lower, too. Credit is never extended, but many casinos have handy credit-card machines that dispense cash for a hefty fee.

Sports and Fitness

All but the smallest ships have at least one pool, some of them elaborate affairs with water slides or retractable roofs; hot tubs and whirlpools are quite common. Pools may be filled with fresh water or salt water; some ships have one of each. While in port or during rough weather, the pools are usually emptied or covered with canvas. Many are too narrow or too short to allow swimmers more than a few strokes in any direction; none have diving boards, and not all are heated. Often there are no lifeguards. Wading pools are sometimes provided for small children.

The top deck is usually called the Sun Deck or Sports Deck. On some ships this is where you'll find the pool or whirlpool; on others it is dedicated to volleyball, table tennis, shuffleboard, and other such sports. A number of ships have paddle-tennis courts, and a few have golf driving ranges. (Skeet shooting is usually offered at the stern of a lower deck.) Often, at twilight or after the sun goes down, the Sun Deck is used for dancing, barbecues, limbo contests, or other social activities.

Most newer ships and some older ones have well-equipped fitness centers, many with massage, sauna, and whirlpools. An upper-deck fitness center often has an airy and sunny view of the sea; an inside, lower-deck health club is often dark and small unless it is equipped with an indoor pool or beauty salon. Many ships have full-service exercise rooms with bodybuilding equipment, stationary bicycles, rowing machines, treadmills, aerobics classes, and personal fitness instruction. Some ships even have structured, cruise-length physical-fitness programs, which may include lectures on weight loss or nutrition. These often are tied in with a spa menu in the dining room. Beauty salons adjacent to the health club may offer spa treatments such as facials and mud wraps. The more extensive programs are often sold on a daily or weekly basis.

GOING ASHORE

Up to eight ships at a time can dock at Bridgetown's Deep Water Harbour, on the northwest side of Carlisle Bay. The snazzy Cruise Ship Terminal has 19 duty-free shops, 13 local retail stores, handicraft vendors, a post office, telephone station, tourist information desk, and a taxi stand. To get downtown, follow the shoreline to the Careenage. By foot, it will take you about 15 minutes, or you can take a cab for $3 each way. The taxi fare to Paradise, Brandon, or Brighton beaches runs $3–$5; to Holetown it's $7. Drivers accept U.S. dollars and appreciate a 10% tip. Taxis operate at a fixed hourly rate of $17.50 per carload (up to three passengers fit comfortably) and will cheerfully narrate a tour.

Shore Excursions

Traveling by cruise ship presents an opportunity to visit many different places in a short time. The flip side is that your stay will be limited in each port of call. For that reason, cruise lines invented shore excursions, which maximize your time by organizing the touring for you, but you will pay more for the convenience of having the ship do the legwork. Of course, you can always book a tour independently, hire a taxi, or use foot power to explore on your own. The following excursions are good choices on Barbados. They may not be offered by all cruise lines. Times and prices are approximate.

ISLAND SIGHTS

Harrison's Cave. After a bus tour of the island's central parishes, passengers board an electric tram for a one-hour tour of this series of limestone caves. A highlight is the 40-ft underground waterfall that plunges into a deep pool. *Duration: 3½ hrs.* ✉ *$32.*

UNDERSEA CREATURES

Atlantis Submarine. A 50-ft sub dives as deep as 150 ft below the surface for an exciting view of Barbados's profuse marine life. Most passengers find this trip to the depths to be a thrilling experience. *Duration: 2 hrs.* ✉ *$80.*

Returning to the Ship

Cruise lines are strict about sailing times, which are posted at the gangway and elsewhere as well as announced in the daily schedule of activities. Be certain to be back on board at least a half hour before the announced sailing time or you may be stranded. If you are on a shore excursion that was sold by the cruise line, however, the captain will wait for your group before casting off. That is one reason many passengers prefer ship-packaged tours.

If you are not on one of the ship's tours and the ship does sail without you, immediately contact the cruise line's port representative, whose name and phone number are often listed on the daily schedule of activities. You may be able to hitch a ride on a pilot boat, though that is unlikely. Passengers who miss the boat must pay their own way to the next port of call.

CRUISE LINES TO CONTACT

Carnival Cruise Lines (✉ Carnival Pl., 3655 N.W. 87th Ave., Miami, FL 33178, ☎ 305/599–2600 or 800/227–6482).

Celebrity Cruises (✉ 5201 Blue Lagoon Dr., Miami, FL 33126, ☎ 800/437–3111).

Club Med (✉ 40 W. 57th St., New York, NY 10019, ☎ 800/258–2633 or 800/453–7447).

Crystal Cruises (✉ 2121 Ave. of the Stars, Los Angeles, CA 90067, ☎ 800/446–6620).

Cunard Line (✉ 555 5th Ave., New York, NY 10017, ☎ 800/528–6273).

Holland America Line (✉ 300 Elliott Ave. W, Seattle, WA 98119, ☎ 800/426–0327).

Norwegian Cruise Line (✉ 95 Merrick Way, Coral Gables, FL 33134, ☎ 800/327–7030).

Princess Cruises (✉ 10100 Santa Monica Blvd., Los Angeles, CA 90067, ☎ 310/553–1770 or 800/421–0522).

Radisson Seven Seas Cruises (✉ 600 Corporate Dr., Suite 410, Fort Lauderdale, FL 33334, ☎ 800/333–3333).

Royal Caribbean International (✉ 1050 Caribbean Way, Miami, FL 33132, ☎ 305/539–6000 or 800/255–4373 for brochures).

Royal Olympic Cruises (✉ 1 Rockefeller Plaza, Suite 325, New York, NY 10020, ☎ 212/397–6400 or 800/872–6400; 800/368–3888 in Canada).

Seawind Cruise Line (✉ 4770 Biscayne Blvd., Suite 700, Miami, FL 33145, ☎ 305/573–3222).

Silversea Cruises (✉ 110 E. Broward Blvd., Fort Lauderdale, FL 33301, ☎ 954/522–4477 or 800/722–9955).

Star Clippers (✉ 4101 Salzedo Ave., Coral Gables, FL 33146, ☎ 800/442–0551).

Windstar Cruises (✉ 300 Elliott Ave. W, Seattle, WA 98119, ☎ 800/258–7245).

INDEX

NOTES

NOTES

NOTES

NOTES

Fodor's Travel Publications

Available at bookstores everywhere, or call 1–800–533–6478, 24 hours a day.

Gold Guides

U.S.

Alaska	Florida	New Orleans	Seattle & Vancouver
Arizona	Hawai'i	New York City	The South
Boston	Las Vegas,	Pacific North Coast	U.S. & British
California	Reno, Tahoe	Philadelphia &	Virgin Islands
Cape Cod, Martha's	Los Angeles	the Pennsylvania	USA
Vineyard, Nantucket	Maine, Vermont,	Dutch Country	Virginia & Maryland
The Carolinas &	New Hampshire	The Rockies	Walt Disney World,
Georgia	Maui & Lāna'i	San Diego	Universal Studios
Chicago	Miami & the Keys	San Francisco	and Orlando
Colorado	New England	Santa Fe, Taos,	Washington, D.C.
		Albuquerque	

Foreign

Australia	Europe	Mexico	Provence &
Austria	Florence, Tuscany	Montréal &	the Riviera
The Bahamas	& Umbria	Québec City	Scandinavia
Belize & Guatemala	France	Moscow, St.	Scotland
Bermuda	Germany	Petersburg, Kiev	Singapore
Canada	Great Britain	The Netherlands,	South Africa
Cancún, Cozumel,	Greece	Belgium &	South America
Yucatán Peninsula	Hong Kong	Luxembourg	Southeast Asia
Caribbean	India	New Zealand	Spain
China	Ireland	Norway	Sweden
Costa Rica	Israel	Nova Scotia,	Switzerland
Cuba	Italy	New Brunswick,	Thailand
The Czech Republic &	Japan	Prince Edward Island	Toronto
Slovakia	London	Paris	Turkey
Eastern &	Madrid & Barcelona	Portugal	Vienna & the Danube
Central Europe			Valley

Special-Interest Guides

Adventures to Imagine	Great American	Kodak Guide to	Walt Disney World
Alaska Ports of Call	Learning Vacations	Shooting Great	for Adults
Ballpark Vacations	Great American	Travel Pictures	Weekends in
Caribbean Ports	Sports & Adventure	National Parks and	New York
of Call	Vacations	Seashores of the East	Wendy Perrin's
The Complete Guide	Great American	National Parks of	Secrets Every Smart
to America's	Vacations	the West	Traveler Should Know
National Parks	Great American	Nights to Imagine	Where Should We
Disney Like a Pro	Vacations for	Rock & Roll Traveler	Take the Kids?
Europe Ports of Call	Travelers with	Great Britain	California
Family Adventures	Disabilities	and Ireland	Where Should We
Fodor's Gay Guide	Halliday's New	Rock & Roll Traveler	Take the Kids?
to the USA	Orleans Food	USA	Northeast
Fodor's How to Pack	Explorer	Sunday in	Worldwide Cruises
	Healthy Escapes	San Francisco	and Ports of Call

Fodor's Special Series

Fodor's Best Bed & Breakfasts

America

California

The Mid-Atlantic

New England

The Pacific Northwest

The South

The Southwest

The Upper Great Lakes

Compass American Guides

Alaska

Arizona

Boston

Chicago

Colorado

Hawai'i

Hollywood

Idaho

Las Vegas

Maine

Manhattan

Minnesota

Montana

New Mexico

New Orleans

Oregon

Pacific Northwest

San Francisco

Santa Fe

South Carolina

South Dakota

Southwest

Texas

Utah

Virginia

Washington

Wine Country

Wisconsin

Wyoming

Citypacks

Amsterdam

Atlanta

Berlin

Chicago

Florence

Hong Kong

London

Los Angeles

Montréal

New York City

Paris

Prague

Rome

San Francisco

Tokyo

Venice

Washington, D.C.

Exploring Guides

Australia

Boston & New England

Britain

California

Canada

Caribbean

China

Costa Rica

Egypt

Florence & Tuscany

Florida

France

Germany

Greek Islands

Hawaii

Ireland

Israel

Italy

Japan

London

Mexico

Moscow & St. Petersburg

New York City

Paris

Prague

Provence

Rome

San Francisco

Scotland

Singapore & Malaysia

South Africa

Spain

Thailand

Turkey

Venice

Flashmaps

Boston

New York

San Francisco

Washington, D.C.

Fodor's Gay Guides

Los Angeles & Southern California

New York City

Pacific Northwest

San Francisco and the Bay Area

South Florida

USA

Pocket Guides

Acapulco

Aruba

Atlanta

Barbados

Budapest

Jamaica

London

New York City

Paris

Prague

Puerto Rico

Rome

San Francisco

Washington, D.C.

Languages for Travelers (Cassette & Phrasebook)

French

German

Italian

Spanish

Mobil Travel Guides

America's Best Hotels & Restaurants

California and the West

Great Lakes

Major Cities

Mid-Atlantic

Northeast

Northwest and Great Plains

Southeast

Southwest and South Central

Rivages Guides

Bed and Breakfasts of Character and Charm in France

Hotels and Country Inns of Character and Charm in France

Hotels and Country Inns of Character and Charm in Italy

Hotels and Country Inns of Character and Charm in Paris

Hotels and Country Inns of Character and Charm in Portugal

Hotels and Country Inns of Character and Charm in Spain

Short Escapes

Britain

France

Near New York City

New England

Fodor's Sports

Golf Digest's Places to Play

Skiing USA

USA Today The Complete Four Sport Stadium Guide

WHEREVER YOU TRAVEL, *H*ELP IS NEVER FAR AWAY.

From planning your trip to

providing travel assistance along

the way, American Express®

Travel Service Offices are

always there to help

you do more.